The MYSTERY and MEANING of the MASS

JOSEPH M. CHAMPLIN

A Crossroad Book
The Crossroad Publishing Company
New York

Imprimatur: Most Reverend Thomas J. Costello, D.D.
Vicar General, Diocese of Syracuse, New York
December 8, 1998

The Crossroad Publishing Company
16 Penn Plaza, 481 Eighth Avenue
New York, NY 10001

Printed in the United States of America

The text of this book is set in 11.5/15.5 Sabon.
The display faces are Cochin and Goudy Old Style.

Library of Congress Cataloging-in-Publication Data
Champlin, Joseph M.
    The mystery and meaning of the Mass / Joseph M. Champlin.– Rev. ed.
       p. cm.
    Includes bibliographical references.
    ISBN 0-8245-2296-6 (alk. paper)
    1. Mass. I. Title.
BX2230.3.C43 2005
264′.0203 – dc22

                                                                    2004028242

To the memory of a mentor of mine,
St. Louis priest Monsignor Martin Hellriegel,
splendid pastor, lover of the liturgy, prophetic teacher,
whose famous demonstrations of the Mass inspired me
nearly a half century ago.

CONTENTS

PREFACE

During my more than four decades in the priestly ministry, I have served as pastor of several parishes. One was a small city church with about 750 households. Another, a large suburban faith community, included 1900 families. The third, my present assignment, is the cathedral for the diocese of Syracuse, a center-city congregation of some 700 households, but with visitors making up half of the weekend worshiping assemblies.

At each of these parishes, I have over two weekends conducted a "demonstration" or "explanation" of the Mass. Carried out during each scheduled eucharistic liturgy, these commentaries outlined the general flow of the Mass and detailed the background or meaning of its components.

The response of parishioners and visitors has always been quite positive. Moreover, after one demonstration, a person in attendance asked if these explanations were in print or, if not, suggested that they be written down and published. Those affirmative reactions and that specific recommendation led to *The Mystery and Meaning of the Mass*.

❖

We might ask, first, what is the origin of the very word "Mass"?

The Latin conclusion of the Mass is "Ite, missa est." That command could be translated in various ways, such as "Go, it is finished," "Go, the Mass is ended," or in a more expressive version, "Go, you are being sent."

The key word here is *missa,* the past participle of the Latin verb *mittere,* which means to send or dismiss. Our contemporary terms "missile" and "missive" spring from that same word.

Eventually the word *missa* meant the entire eucharistic celebration and, after passing through various other vernacular languages, surfaced in English as "Mass."

The English versions of this conclusion or dismissal, as it occurs in eucharistic liturgies since 1970 are "Go in the peace of Christ"; "The Mass is ended, go in peace"; or "Go in peace to love and serve the Lord." The Latin text, however, retains "Ite, missa est."

In Latin or English the basic meaning remains the same. Having been nurtured by the Word of God and nourished by the body and blood of Christ, we are sent out, missioned, to bring the good news, the gospel, to others.

While preparing this book and working through the rich intricacies of the Mass, I found that the study, reflection, and writing have positively overflowed into my own celebration of the Eucharist day after day. It has made me more conscious of deeper meanings already known or just discovered, and thus helped me celebrate this great mystery a little better.

In a superb volume, *Why I Am Still a Catholic*, Kevin and Marilyn Ryan have gathered essays responding to that question by twenty-five well-known people. In a remarkable number of instances, authors cite the Mass as the central reason why they are now still members of the Catholic Church. Novelist Jon Hasler is one of those persons. He writes:

> I'm still a Catholic because I love the Mass. It punctuates my life like a semicolon; it's a pause, a breather, in my week, my day. I don't pray very well at Mass; in fact, I often don't pay much attention, yet sixty years of churchgoing has left me with a need — it's more than mere habit; it's a deep-seated need — to be lifted up and carried along, time after time, by the familiar words and rubrics. It's like boarding a boat and standing out from the shore of my life for a half-hour or so, viewing it through the refreshing air of a calm and scenic harbor.[1]

No wonder many view the Mass as their dominant motivation for remaining Catholic. For the Mass is a mystery, an awesome action by which, through Christ's power, a priest transforms human materials into divine elements, changing bread and wine into Jesus' body and blood.

However, in every eucharistic liturgy there are also many obscure or almost hidden gestures, often unfamiliar words, and moments of silence broken by vocal responses. These contribute to a mysteriousness surrounding this religious service.

Many Catholics, even well instructed ones, and others not Roman Catholic pose questions like: Why does the priest kiss the altar or pour water into the cup? What are the reasons behind touching our face at the Gospel or striking our breasts before Communion?

I hope this book will answer most of these inquiries about the many external elements of the Mass. In doing so, it should eliminate some of the mysteriousness that surrounds our eucharistic ritual. Still, I pray that these pages will at the same time deepen each reader's understanding, appreciation, and love for the fundamental mystery of the Mass itself.

PART ONE

THE MYSTERY
OF THE
MASS

CHAPTER ONE

The Center of the Christian Life

The lived-out love for the Mass evident among so many Catholic clergy and laypersons silently speaks volumes about the dignity of the eucharistic celebration. Their examples merely underscore what official documents teach abstractly about this most sacred action of Christ and the church. Those texts declare that the Mass is "the center of the Christian life for both the universal and the local church, as well as for each of the faithful."[2]

Examples among the Clergy

About a century ago, a pregnant German woman walked forty-seven miles without food or water to the Shrine of the Precious Blood at Walburn in Germany. She prayed for a safe delivery and a healthy child. However, this devout mother stayed on another day, asking God further that if the child was a boy, he would eventually become a priest. Upon her return, she gave birth to Martin Hellriegel. He did years later enter the seminary, received ordination to the priesthood, and began serving in the United States.

Father Hellriegel spent over two decades as chaplain for the Precious Blood Sisters in O'Fallon, Missouri. During that period, he read widely about church matters and prepared himself for a future day when he would pastor a parish. During the 1940s he assumed this responsibility, shepherding the people of Holy Cross Church in the Baden section of St. Louis. However, those years of research and his love for the sacred liturgy also led him to a leadership role in the Liturgical Conference, a pioneering movement that helped prompt the worship changes of the Second Vatican Council.

A final Christmas letter to his friends included a statement he had made countless times over the phone or in person: "I can assure you that the grace to offer the Divine Sacrifice was and ever will be the sunshine of my priestly life."

Despite total blindness over the last half dozen years of his life, Monsignor Hellriegel continued to celebrate and preach at daily Mass. He had memorized the liturgy's fixed parts and arranged for readers to proclaim in English the assigned variable biblical texts. To the very end, the Mass was indeed the sunshine of his life.[3]

❖

The mother of widely read author Father Henri Nouwen lived about a half century after Mrs. Hellriegel. But they both possessed the identical deep faith and fervent devotion. Writing after his mother's death, Nouwen noted that there were few days in her adult life that she did not go to Mass and Communion. The Eucharist, he maintains, was "the center of her life." Wherever she happened to be or whatever she was doing, Mrs. Nouwen sought out a nearby church where she could participate in the Eucharist. This desire led her husband to arrange his many business trips with her in such a fashion that they could together attend Mass.

Her great devotion to the Eucharist was, in Nouwen's judgment, perhaps the main factor in his decision to become a priest. Moreover, her example understandably influenced the way Father Nouwen lived out his priesthood. Because of his popularity and reputation as a teacher, speaker, and writer, many might have considered that celebrating Mass was not high on Nouwen's priority list. Quite the contrary, he writes that "the Eucharist is the center of my life and everything else received its meaning from that center.... For me, to be a priest means to be ordained to present Christ every day in food and drink to my fellow Christians."[4]

❖

Bishop Eugene Gerber made a dream of his into a reality. On the outskirts of Wichita, he oversaw the construction of the Catholic Care Center for the elderly and retirees, including several dozen priests, and the Spiritual Life Center for retreats and conferences.

On the sacristy wall next to the chapel in the Spiritual Life Center is a plaque with these words of exhortation: "Offer this Mass as if it were your first Mass, your last Mass, and your only Mass." Priests preparing there for the Eucharist cannot avoid seeing that admonition. It reminds them of what they are about: celebrating the central act of worship in the Catholic tradition.

EXAMPLES AMONG LAYPERSONS

For Catholics, attendance at Sunday Mass continues to be a serious obligation. But there is no requirement to participate in weekday Eucharists. That makes the large number of people at daily Masses a remarkable testimony to their high regard for the Eucharist. This testimony is even more impressive when the churches are located in resort areas and the majority of worshipers are tourists or vacationers.

St. Augustine's Church on Oahu in the Hawaiian Islands; Stella Maris Chapel in the Condado section of San Juan, Puerto Rico; St. Ann's Community at Bethany Beach on the Delaware Shore of the Atlantic — these three churches, separated by thousands of miles, share similar experiences: a substantial number of communicants for their weekday Masses, some at early morning hours and others in the late afternoon.

❖

Thanksgiving is not a holy day of obligation for Roman Catholics in the United States. But for many parishes throughout the land, carefully prepared Masses on this holiday draw capacity crowds.

Appropriate music, a procession with food donations for the poor, and a reflective homily on the past year's blessings surely contribute to the attractiveness of these celebrations. But the essential element is the Eucharist, giving thanks for God's gifts, expressing in the best possible way our gratitude for the Lord's many favors through participation in the Mass on that day.

❖

Dorothy Day and Mother Teresa of Calcutta shared a common concern for the poorest of the poor. But they also practiced a similar priority in their lives — getting to Mass every day.

The two of them met in Calcutta: Dorothy Day, committed to living in poverty so that she might better serve the poor in New York City; Mother Teresa, dedicated to living simply and prayerfully so that she and her sisters might more effectively serve the poor throughout the world.

One founded the Catholic Worker Community, the other the Missionaries of Charity. But for "each one the Mass was the central act of the day. Despite her schedule of travel, Dorothy Day hardly ever missed daily Mass."[5] Mother Teresa made daily Eucharist an essential part of her religious community's rule of life and, of course, observed that directive.

OFFICIAL CHURCH TEACHING

The exemplary actions of these clergy and laypersons flow from constant church teaching about the dignity of the Mass. At the Second Vatican Council during the early 1960s, the bishops gathered at Rome taught in the *Constitution on the Sacred Liturgy* that the liturgy,

> especially in the divine sacrifice of the Eucharist, is supremely effective in enabling the faithful to express in their lives and portray to others the mystery of Christ and the real nature of the true church. ... The liturgy daily builds up those who are in the church, making of them a holy temple of the Lord, a dwelling place for God in the Spirit.[6]

Later in that document, the chapter entitled "The Sacred Mystery of the Eucharist" further describes in detail the marvelous nature of the Mass and outlines changes in its structure to facilitate greater participation by the faithful in eucharistic celebrations.[7]

❖

We cited at the beginning of this chapter words from the *General Instruction* of the revised *Roman Missal* published in 1969. *The New Order of Mass*, authorized four hundred years after the introduction of the *Roman Missal* developed by the Council of Trent, contains an introductory chapter on the "Importance and Dignity of the Eucharistic Celebration."[8]

❖

The *Catechism of the Catholic Church*, published by Pope John Paul II in 1992, treats the Mass in Part Two, "The Celebration of the Christian Mystery," under article 3, "The Sacrament of the Eucharist." It states that the Eucharist is the source and summit of the Christian life; that the other sacraments are bound up with the Eucharist and oriented toward it; that through the Mass we already unite ourselves with the heavenly liturgy and anticipate eternal life; that "the Eucharist is the sum and summary of our faith."[9]

The example of the clergy, the attitude of laypersons, and official church teaching concur on this point: the sublime dignity of the Mass, or Eucharist.

CHAPTER TWO

CHANGELESS AND
CHANGEABLE ELEMENTS

Diamonds are forever, the advertisement proclaims. But the circular bands and curved settings that hold them are not. Over many years the band often wears thin and the decorative setting usually loses some of its beauty. They both may require repair, refurbishing, or replacement. But in this renewal process, jewelers do not discard the diamond itself. They merely enhance its surroundings. That example may help, by analogy, to understand the past history and ongoing development of the Mass ritual.

At the Second Vatican Council, the bishops clearly distinguished between changeless and changeable elements in the Mass structure. As they explained their desire for a careful, but general restoration of the liturgy, these church leaders noted:

The liturgy is made up of unchangeable elements divinely instituted, and of elements subject to change. These latter not only may be changed but ought to be changed with the passage of time, if they have suffered from the intrusion of anything out of harmony with the inner nature of the liturgy or have become less suitable.[10]

In succeeding paragraphs, the bishops warned that there be no change simply for the sake of change, and any new development must grow "organically" from existing forms:

There must be no innovations unless the good of the Church genuinely and certainly requires them, and care must be taken that any new forms adopted should in some way grow organically from forms already existing.[11]

CHANGELESS ELEMENTS

What are these unchangeable, essential, and changeless elements? Since the Mass perfectly reenacts the Last Supper and re-presents in an unbloody manner the actions of Holy Thursday, Good Friday, and Easter Sunday, we naturally look to the biblical accounts of this final sacred meal for guidance. In the earliest written account of the Last Supper, Paul describes the event in this way:

I received from the Lord what I also handed on to you, that the Lord Jesus, on the night he was handed over, took bread, and after he had given thanks, broke it and said, "This is my body that is for you. Do this in remembrance of me." In the same way also the cup, after supper, saying, "This cup is the new covenant in my blood. Do this, as often as you drink it, in remembrance of me."

(1 Cor. 11:23–25)

Similar, but later, descriptions occur in the Gospels of Matthew (26:26–29), Mark (14:22–25), and Luke (22: 14–20). Bread, wine, Jesus' words of institution, and participants receiving in Communion the consecrated particles, therefore, seem the obviously essential and unchangeable elements.

But even here we have some contemporary confusion in the discussion. The church today has allowed a substitute instead of wine for those struggling with an alcohol addiction. Moreover, it permits a special form of bread for those allergic to gluten. Nevertheless, those four ingredients would seem to be the irreplaceable and changeless items of the Mass.

Early accounts of the Mass, or Eucharist, describe how the first Christians expanded this fundamental ritual, surrounding it with suitable prayers and gestures. The *Didache* at the end of the first century reveals the understandably strong Jewish influence upon the way those first Christians celebrated Mass.

However, it was St. Justin, a philosopher and martyr writing about 150, who described the expanded version of the Mass in use at that time:

And on that day which is called after the sun, all who are in the towns and in the country gather together for a communal celebration. And then the memoirs of the Apostles or the writings of the Prophets are read, as long as time permits. After the reader has finished his task, the one presiding gives an address, urgently admonishing his hearers to practice these beautiful teachings in their lives. Then all stand up together and recite prayers. After the end of the prayers, as has already been remarked above, the bread and wine mixed with water are brought, and the president offers up prayers and thanksgivings, as much as in him lies. The people chime in with an Amen. Then takes place the distribution, to all attending, of the things over which the thanksgiving had been spoken, and the deacons bring a portion to the absent. Besides, those who are well-to-do give whatever they will. What is gathered is deposited with the one presiding, who therewith helps orphans and widows.[12]

In the ensuing centuries, an enormous variety of prayers, gestures, and objects found their way into the Mass, some appropriate, some not so proper.

Changeable Elements

Centuries of scholarly research, sporadic official changes, some minor and other major, and the constant advocacy of the liturgical movement in the first half of the twentieth century prepared the way for and culminated in the work of the Second Vatican Council.

Second Vatican Council

On December 4, 1963, the bishops gathered in Rome published the *Constitution on the Sacred Liturgy*. Its call for active participation in the liturgy by all participants and for those changes in the rituals needed to achieve that involvement charted the course for the church's worship during the second half of the twentieth century.

The centerpieces of these changes were the *Sacramentary* for *The New Order of Mass* and the *Lectionary* of biblical readings for worship services. The *Sacramentary* provided some two thousand prayers for Sundays, weekdays, and a wide variety of special occasions. The *Lectionary* opened up more richly the treasures of the Bible by offering a three-year cycle of Sunday readings, a two-year cycle for weekdays, and a vast assortment of biblical excerpts for different situations.

New Millennium

That change process continues on into our day, the new millennium of the twenty-first century.

Major documents have and will continue to influence the way we celebrate Mass through the decades ahead.

- A four-volume *Lectionary for Mass* "For Use in the Dioceses of the United States of America: Second

Typical Edition," published by the United States Conference of Catholic Bishops in the initial years of this century, is the authorized, standard text for all weekday and Sunday Masses in this country.

• These three documents have made additional modifications in the actions of the Mass: *General Instruction of the Roman Missal* (third edition) in 2003, *Introduction to the Order of Mass: A Pastoral Resource of the Bishop's Committee on the Liturgy* (2003), and *Instruction on the Eucharist* (2004).

• A revised *Sacramentary* is under construction and its ultimate arrival will alter the wording of prayers at Mass.

This book will for the most part analyze the Mass as it is in the present, with an occasional glance at the past, and perhaps a hint of what we might expect in the future.

CHAPTER THREE

Plan of the Mass

Monsignor Martin Hellriegel, mentioned earlier, developed during that same midcentury era a practical explanation of the then current Mass format. His famous "demonstrations" presented a simple and understandable description of the eucharistic celebration. His concepts and words also established a foundation for grasping the developments that were to come a few years later in 1970. The German-born St. Louis pastor used the image of two mountains, each with an ascending and descending slope, to communicate the basic movement of the Mass.

Two Mountains

The first and lesser mountain consists of the various prayers and biblical readings during the initial part of the Holy Sacrifice. On the ascending slope, we speak to God; on the descending slope, God speaks to us.

After we together prepare our hearts and praise God in the Gloria, the priest collects our keenly felt but unspoken petitions and offers them to God. We thus, as it were, speak to God.

The Most Holy Trinity, in response, speaks to us on the downward slope of this lesser mountain. First, the Father addresses us in the Old Testament and New Testament passages. Next, the Son communicates to us through the Gospel. Finally, the Holy Spirit employs words of the homily (then called a sermon) to touch the hearts of the gathered assembly.

We conclude this first mountain, having heard God speak to us, by expressing our acceptance of and belief in the Lord's words through reciting or singing the Creed.

On the second and greater mountain, we give to God on the ascending slope; on the descending slope, God gives to us. This mountain consists of those three principal parts of offertory, consecration, and Communion.

Gathering the gifts, preparing them, and presenting these inner offerings (our hearts) and outer offerings (the bread and wine) to God take us from the offertory to the consecration. At that point, the priest's words and actions transform these gifts into the body and blood of Christ.

The ascending slope continues, however, as the priest in our name offers to the Father this most precious gift of Jesus the Son. The postconsecration prayers are considered most powerful since we are presenting not merely our human offerings but the divine Christ to God on high in the Holy Spirit. The Trinitarian doxology concludes this upward movement.

The Our Father serves as a kind of bridge between the ascending and descending slopes. The first half of the Lord's prayer in a sense honors God; the second half articulates our needs. We ask God to give us, forgive us, protect us.

On that downward slope, God does indeed give to us, feeding those who come to the table with Christ's body and blood in Communion.

Having heard the Lord speak to us on the first mountain and having received Jesus himself on the second mountain, with the Mass finished we are directed to go in peace. The presiding priest in effect sends us forth to bring Christ and his message to others.

MASS OF 1970

This image of two mountains establishes a basis for understanding the approach enshrined within *The New Order of Mass* introduced in 1970. The *General Instruction of the Roman Missal,* implementing the directives of the Second Vatican Council, placed the structure of the Mass in a quite different perspective, although one that echoes the two mountains conceived by Monsignor Hellriegel.

In the words of the *General Instruction,* the Mass contains "two parts, namely, the liturgy of the Word and the liturgy of the Eucharist, which are so closely connected with each other that they constitute one act of worship."[13] During the Mass, therefore, we have two tables, the table of God's Word and the table of the body of Christ. They both provide instruction and nourishment for faithful worshipers. Certain other rites initiate the eucharistic celebration and conclude it.[14]

The bishops at the Second Vatican Council taught that, since these two parts are so closely connected with each other that they form one single act of worship, pastors of souls should strongly urge parishioners to take part in the entire Mass, especially on Sundays.[15]

EXTERNAL CHANGES

This fundamental shift in the plan of the Mass to those two focal points, the Liturgy of the Word and the Liturgy of the Eucharist, generated several significant changes in church architecture, ritual books, and liturgical actions.

Architecture. Prior to the Second Vatican Council the size, placement, and style of the ambo (formerly called lectern or pulpit) in Catholic churches often tended to distinguish or separate it from the altar. After the introduction of *The New Order of Mass*, the ambo in new or restored sanctuaries generally is nearer the altar and usually similar in materials and design. This architectural change reflects the close link that now exists between Word and Eucharist.

Ritual Books. Prior to the Second Vatican Council, one book, the *Roman Missal,* contained all the prayers and readings needed for any Mass. *The New Order of Mass,* on the other hand, with an extraordinarily numerous and rich array of biblical readings and presidential prayers, requires two bound ritual books: The *Lectionary* of Scripture texts and the *Sacramentary* of altar prayers.

Liturgical Actions. Prior to the Second Vatican Council, the priest proclaimed the readings, the preacher usually began and concluded his words with a dramatic sign of the cross, the sermon frequently did not relate to the assigned Scripture, and there seldom were candles by the pulpit.

With the introduction of *The New Order of Mass,* lay persons, or at least readers other than the priest presider, proclaim all the biblical texts except the Gospel, ideally with as many lectors as there are readings.

The church discourages preachers from using the sign of the cross before and after their presentations. This gesture tends to separate the sermon from the Mass rather than visually demonstrating that the homily should flow out of the Scripture proclamation and lead back into the Mass ritual.

"Homily" is the preferred word today instead of "sermon." While the message need not, indeed should not, be a mere retelling or exegesis of the designated readings, the preacher nevertheless must in some way connect his words with the proclaimed biblical passages.

Many churches place two large candles on either side of the ambo with two others by the altar. Some parishes, instead, after completion of the Liturgy of the Word, move the ambo candles to either side of the altar for the Liturgy of the Eucharist. Both arrangements demonstrate the close bond between the table of the Word and the table of the Eucharist.

PRESENT PLAN

The New Order of Mass divides eucharistic celebrations into four parts: Introductory Rites, Liturgy of the Word, Liturgy of the Eucharist, and Concluding Rites. Part II will observe that pattern, explaining in detail the component elements of each section. We will mainly focus on the meaning behind a particular action or object in the Mass, although sometimes describing its historical background and occasionally pointing out possible future changes or developments.

PART TWO

THE MEANING

OF THE

MASS

CHAPTER FOUR

Introductory Rites

The purpose of these rites is to establish community among the assembled faithful and to dispose them to hear the Word of God rightly and to celebrate the Eucharist worthily.[16]

Entrance

On most weekend Masses in most parishes, the presiding priest and altar assistants begin the entrance procession from a location near the main doors of the church. Usually, but not always or necessarily, all assembled join in an appropriate song. The joint singing helps to weld as one those gathered for worship, to direct their attention to the mystery of the feast, season, or event being celebrated, and to accompany this movement to the sanctuary.

KISSING THE ALTAR

After a reverent genuflection or bow to the tabernacle and/or altar, the priest (and deacon, if there is one) kisses the altar.

The church has traditionally viewed the altar as a symbol of Christ and the center of the church. Moreover, during the Middle Ages, because of an increase in devotion to martyrs who gave their lives for the Lord and a desire to enlist their prayerful help or intercession, the custom developed of placing relics from certain saints in the altar itself. For example, the new altar in our cathedral renovated a dozen years ago contains a relic of St. John Neuman, the recently canonized archbishop of Philadelphia, and of St. Catherine Labouré, visionary nineteenth-century French Sister of Charity who walked in the footsteps of St. Vincent de Paul.

The kiss, therefore, is a special and solemn gesture of reverence for Christ, for the relics of his special followers enshrined in the altar, and for this holy place at which the sacred mysteries will soon be celebrated.

INCENSATION

On solemn occasions the priest may incense the altar immediately after kissing it. That gesture, repeated several times later in the Mass (before the Gospel, during the preparation of the gifts, and during the institution narrative, or consecration), has biblical origins and occurs in many religious traditions. It symbolizes our prayer rising to God on high; it adds solemnity to the celebration; it expresses honor and respect for the object incensed.

Procession to the Presiding Chair

After reverencing and perhaps incensing the altar, the priest and deacon proceed to the presidential, or presiding, chair. Both the Introductory and Concluding Rites take place at this location. While avoiding the appearance of a throne, the chair still should be dignified, distinct from other sanctuary chairs and at a suitable spot where the priest can preside over the people and lead them in prayer.

Sign of the Cross

The most common identifying gesture for Roman Catholics worldwide is the sign of the cross. On televised events we watch professional athletes sign themselves at significant moments in a contest. Many Catholics often do so immediately after receiving Communion. The sign of the cross generally accompanies grace at meals, prayer before class, and the blessing of objects.

It is therefore most natural, expected, and even necessary that the priest and the entire congregation, having gathered together before the altar, begin by making the sign of the cross, with the presider articulating the familiar words.

The priest celebrant in the previous Mass ritual made this sign of the cross over fifty times. The spiritual thinking in that era presumably argued that repetition enhanced the meaning of a gesture. The 1970 format simplifies this procedure. It requires the sign of the cross only three times — at the beginning of Mass, over the gifts, and at the end (plus one other time in Eucharistic Prayer I). The thinking in our era would argue that making this gesture fewer times, but perhaps with greater care and reverence, is more effective.

The words and gesture that form the sign of the cross express our major Christian mysteries. We believe in one God (in the "name" not "names") and three Persons — Father, Son, and Holy Spirit. The cross itself recalls Calvary, the crucifixion, the dying of Jesus for us. But before Christ could do this on our behalf, he first had to enter our world through the birth at Christmas. And we never stop at Good Friday, but move on through Holy Saturday to Easter and the Resurrection. Consequently, and usually unconsciously, we manifest through the spoken and acted-out sign of the cross faith in the oneness of God, the Trinity, the Incarnation, and Redemption.

GREETING

Following the sign of the cross, the priest addresses all those present with a formal greeting. The ritual provides three alternatives. We might term them Apostolic

Greetings since they follow the example of St. Paul and are texts that he employed in his various letters.

The grace of our Lord Jesus Christ and the love of God and the fellowship of the Holy Spirit be with you all.

The grace and peace of God our Father and the Lord Jesus Christ be with you.

The Lord be with you.

The people respond: "And also with you."[17]

Jesus taught that where two or three people gather in his name, he is there in the midst of them (Matt. 18:20). The bishops at the Second Vatican Council echoed and expanded upon that teaching. Paragraph 7 of their *Constitution on the Sacred Liturgy* establishes the doctrinal foundation for all subsequent liturgical changes. It states that "Christ is always present in his church, especially in liturgical celebrations." After listing in staccato fashion several ways in which the Risen Jesus is present, it concludes: "Lastly, he is present when the Church prays or sings."[18] This initial greeting and response help both priest and the assembled to acknowledge these truths about Jesus' presence and to be inspired by them.

WELCOME

At this time, the priest in an informal way may welcome strangers, guests, and special groups, with a particular word to children when a significant number of them have gathered for the Mass. He also, in carefully prepared comments, introduces the theme or themes of the Eucharist about to be celebrated. These welcoming and introductory efforts set a tone, atmosphere, and orientation for everything that follows.

PENITENTIAL RITE

The priest, having just functioned as a community builder, now shifts to another role as a leader of reflective silence and expressed repentance. This tension of moving back and forth from the community dimension of worship to its transcendent character, from sound to silence to sound, from individual pondering to communal praying, arises frequently during the Mass. The priest needs wisdom, tact, and confidence to do this well.

Using supplied formulas or his own words, he begins by inviting participants to call to mind their sins and to ask the gentle, compassionate God for pardon, forgiveness, and strength. The ritual supposes that there follows "a pause for silent reflection."[19]

Over the past quarter century since the introduction of the new Mass, my experience has been that this pause generally is minimal or nonexistent. Furthermore, it is so brief that assembled worshipers often are not exactly certain what they should do or think during that moment of silence.

We respond in three ways:

"I Confess." The 1570 Mass always began in Latin with the "Confiteor" and included the famous triple beating of one's breast to the words "Mea culpa, mea culpa, mea maxima culpa" ("through my fault, through my fault, through my most grievous fault"). The 1970 version is modified, with only one striking of the breast and an adjusted English text: "I have sinned through my own fault (strike breast) in my thoughts and in my words, in what I have done and in what I have failed to do."[20]

Penitential Psalm Verses. "Lord, we have sinned against you: Lord, have mercy." "Lord, show us your mercy and love: And grant us your salvation."[21]

Litany of Praise for God's Mercy. The priest addresses these triple invocations to Christ that include a title, attribute, or action of Jesus. The assembly responds: "Lord, have mercy.... Christ, have mercy.... Lord, have mercy." For example:

"You were sent to heal the contrite."
"Lord have mercy."

"You came to call sinners."
"Christ have mercy."

"You plead for us at the right hand of the Father."
"Lord have mercy."

The *Sacramentary* provides eight formulas for this litany, but offers the opportunity for the priest (or parish liturgical advisors) to create additional ones.[22] However, these creative versions should be a litany of praise to Christ and not a litany of our own faults. For example:

Lord Jesus, you often retired to deserted places and
prayed . . . [*appropriate*]

For the times we have failed to pray . . . [*inappropriate*]

The latter, inappropriate type has become common in the
United States.

The priest concludes all of these forms with, "May
almighty God have mercy on us, forgive us our sins, and
bring us to everlasting life."[23]

To experience God's great love and forgiveness we first
must recognize our sins and shortcomings, tasting the
pain that goes with those faults and failings. Then we
need to believe, to have faith that the Lord's mercy is
more than a match for our mistakes. The Penitential Rite
helps us foster those attitudes within us at the start of
Mass. The Penitential Rite may be said or sung, and during Lent the people may kneel as a further sign of their
inner repentance.

KYRIE

A sort of litany for mercy follows, unless it has already
occurred, particularly in the third version of the Penitential Rite. The people repeat each invocation after the
priest, leader, or choir:

> Lord, have mercy.
> Christ, have mercy.
> Lord, have mercy.

The root meaning of "mercy" goes beyond forgiveness of sins and embraces all of God's blessings.

This litany may likewise be prayed in the original Greek, which found its way into the Roman Mass around the fifth century:

> Kyrie eleison.
> Christe eleison.
> Kyrie eleison.[24]

The Kyrie is by nature a chant and therefore normally sung by the entire congregation alternating with the leader of song or choir. Despite a general absence for many years, the ancient Gregorian chant versions of the Kyrie will usually strike responsive chords in all members of the assembly, young and old.

BLESSING AND SPRINKLING OF WATER

God has used water throughout history to save human beings and in particular to free the Chosen People. The stories of Creation, Noah's Ark, deliverance from pagan bondage through the waters of the Red Sea, water in the desert from a rock, John the Baptist at the Jordan River, and Jesus' words to Nicodemus that "no one can enter the kingdom of God without being born of water and Spirit" (John 3:5) are but a few examples.

The Catholic Church closely connects baptismal fonts and blessed water. The "holy" water in receptacles at church entrances and with which those entering sign themselves not only signifies spiritual cleansing, but also recalls sacramental baptism, which brings the new life in Christ to the recepient.

To dramatize these connections, the Mass ritual provides for the blessing and sprinkling of water as an occasional replacement for the Penitential Rite and Kyrie. Because this action especially reminds us of baptism and Easter, the blessing and sprinkling ceremony is particularly appropriate during the Easter season.

There are three alternative formulas for the blessing, including one specifically for the Easter season. All of them express gratitude for the gift of water, seek liberation from sin, and recall the graces of baptism.

When the congregation can clearly see the baptismal font, the priest may perform the blessing at that location. He subsequently sprinkles himself and his ministers, and then may move through the church for the sprinkling of the people. To make this action and its meaning clearer, the church recommends that the priest use an abundant amount of water. Some employ the branch of a pine tree and a large basin to achieve that purpose.

Upon completion of this rite, the presiding priest proclaims a prayer that speaks of cleansing from sin and anticipates the Eucharist to come.[25] He continues Mass with the Gloria or Opening Prayer as the season dictates.

There are other adjustments in the Introductory Rites when, for example, a baptism, marriage, or funeral occurs during the Mass.

GLORIA

One of the main stained-glass windows in the apse of our century-old cathedral portrays the birth of Christ at Bethlehem. Hovering over the scene are two angels with an unfolded banner proclaiming, "Gloria in excelsis Deo." Parishioners quickly recognize the phrase, the scene, and the meaning of the words, even when sung in Latin. "Glory to God in the highest..." is meant to be a festive hymn particularly appropriate during the Christmas and Easter seasons. Ideally it should be sung, but nevertheless may be recited, although it is omitted during Advent or Lent.

In this ancient and venerable hymn, the community assembled in faith gives glory to the Father, to Jesus the Lamb of God, and to the Holy Spirit, while at the same time seeking forgiveness and a response to our petitions.[26]

OPENING PRAYER

The priest concludes these diverse and complicated Introductory Rites with an invitation: "Let us pray." A rubric, or instruction, in the ritual states quite simply, but with great ramifications: "Priest and people pray silently for a while."[27]

The Mass before 1970 tended to be a generally "silent" Eucharist in terms of people's responses, yet there were no rubrical regulations calling for such silence. The Mass of 1970, on the other hand, sometimes criticized for

being too "noisy," contains rubrics that on several occasions, as here, direct the worshiping community to pause
for a period of silence. In its introduction, the *Sacramentary* even includes a paragraph explicitly dedicated to
"Silence." Its opening sentence reads: "Silence should be
observed at designated times as part of the celebration."[28]
The balance of that paragraph lists those occasions when
silence is expected.

Even after more than twenty-five years, this invitation and silent pause still seem unclear and unproductive
for most worshiping communities. First of all, the priest
may barely pause before reciting or singing the Opening
Prayer. Even with a significant pause for silent prayer,
however, given our rushed, hurry-up-and-eat culture,
many people wonder what they are supposed to do at
this point or question if the priest has lost his place.

A careful and meaningful invitation to pray coupled
with a substantial pause for silence are critical for this
experience to be effective. The *Sacramentary* prints an
optional addition to the "Let us pray" for Sundays and
major celebrations that can help clarify the purpose of
the silence.

Ideally during this pause, both the priest and the people
become more conscious that they are standing in God's
presence and pray in their hearts for their individualized
intentions or concerns. After that significant pause, the
priest gathers together, or "collects," all those keenly felt
but unspoken petitions and presents them to God. In the
past this prayer was customarily termed the "Collect"
precisely because of that function.

While saying this prayer, the priest extends his hands and lifts them up in an "orans," or praying position. God, of course, is everywhere. Still, with our human limitations we often think of the Lord as being above, "up there," beyond us. The outstretched arms consequently symbolize our prayers of pleading directed heavenward, but also our willingness and need to receive back from on high God's response to these petitions.

The *Sacramentary* contains approximately two thousand prayers of this nature for Mass. That includes, naturally, Sunday Eucharist, but also weekdays, celebrations of saints, ritual Masses like weddings and funerals, and a wide variety of other occasions. It is safe to say that few priests and parish worship teams in the United States have even begun to tap into this rich resource. Church regulations not only allow but strongly encourage full use of these texts to serve the pastoral needs of particular situations. These prayers can be extremely powerful for a gathered group in unique circumstances. For example, at a special Mass for the sick, we pray: "Hear us as we ask your loving help for the sick; restore their health, that they may again offer joyful thanks in your church."[29]

The Opening Prayer concludes in a Trinitarian way with the priest joining his hands as he directs our petitions to the Father through Christ the Son in the Holy Spirit.

The people's response to this prayer is "Amen," a word from the Jewish tradition that expresses solemn ratification, hearty approval, or total agreement: "Yes. So be it. Let it be done. I agree. We concur."

We have gathered together, assembled in faith, prepared our hearts for what is to come, and expressed our needs. In effect we have ascended the slope of that first mountain and spoken to God. Now we sit down, awaiting the Lord's response. God does speak to us in the Liturgy of the Word, which begins immediately.

CHAPTER FIVE

LITURGY OF THE WORD

Readings from Scripture and the chants between the readings form the main part of the liturgy of the word. The homily, profession of faith, and General Intercessions, or Prayer of the Faithful, develop and complete it. In the readings, God speaks to his people of the mystery of salvation and nourishes their spirit; Christ is present through his word. The homily then explains the readings, and the chants and profession of faith comprise the acceptance of God's word. Finally, moved by this word, they pray in the General Intercessions for the needs of the Church and the world.[30]

The liturgy of the Mass now moves from the presidential chair to the ambo for the Liturgy of the Word. As we have already mentioned, many churches today place lighted candles at either side of the ambo to symbolize and highlight Christ's presence in the Word being proclaimed.

Current church directions dictate that the ambo be somewhat elevated, fixed, and of a suitable design to manifest its harmonious and close relationship with the altar. So that people can hear well and pay attention to the Scriptures being proclaimed, the ambo should be of sufficient size and should have adequate lighting and suitable amplification equipment. This distinctive ambo is used for the readings and the responsorial psalm, but may also be employed for the homily and General Intercessions. However, a commentator or leader of song preferably does not stand at the ambo.[31]

The bishops at the Second Vatican Council acknowledged Christ's unique presence in the biblical excerpts proclaimed at Mass: "He is present in his word since it is he himself who speaks when the holy Scriptures are read in Mass."[32]

❖

Several visual signs and liturgical norms underscore the importance and dignity of the biblical words. The church directs that the books from which readers proclaim the scriptural texts should be "worthy, dignified and beautiful." Anxious lectors may feel more comfortable using leaflets, pastoral aids, or missalettes. However, these less permanent and distinctive, more temporary and functional items detract from the sublime nature of God's word.[33] Regulations also prohibit omitting and shortening the biblical text or replacing the sacred words with nonbiblical readings.

The Book of Gospels ideally is bound in an exceptional manner. The minister carries this volume during the entrance procession, holding it at about eye level, and places it upon the altar until needed for the proclamation at the ambo. Afterward, it should rest on a support in a visual place of prominence near the altar for the rest of Mass.

The priest or deacon transfers in a slow-paced procession the Gospel Book, again held high, from the altar to the ambo prior to proclamation of the good news. At the conclusion of this movement, the proclaimer places it at the arranged spot clearly in view of all.

"The Word of the Lord," deliberately said or sung following a brief pause at the end of the first one or two biblical proclamations, should elicit from all this strong phrase of gratitude: "Thanks be to God."

Several well-trained, carefully prepared, and properly motivated lectors, preferably different ones for each reading, proclaim the assigned texts. On solemn occasions, the priest or deacon may incense the Gospel Book just prior to proclaiming the biblical text.

❖

Masses celebrated for the first seven decades of the last century naturally included biblical readings. However, they were somewhat limited with, for example, a one-year-only cycle of Sunday readings and an equally sparse collection of scriptural excerpts for other celebrations.

The bishops at the Vatican Council decreed that in the reform of the Mass those in charge should seek to provide worshipers with "more ample, more varied and more suitable readings" at every Mass. They were to open the treasures of the Bible "more lavishly." These biblical and liturgical scholars were to organize the series of readings so that in the course of several years the faithful would hear a more representative part of the Sacred Scriptures.[34]

The *Ordo Lectionum Missae*, published in 1969 and then translated and introduced in the United States on the First Sunday of Advent 1971, carried out all those directives. Catholics in our nation since then have grown accustomed to this incredibly rich and useful volume with its collection of biblical excerpts.

In 1981 the Holy See issued in Latin a second so-called "typical" edition of the *Lectionary*. There were changes and additions, but of a relatively minor nature. However, translation of this version into English became a complex, lengthy, and controverted process. The second edition of the *Lectionary for Mass for Use in the Dioceses of the United States of America* was eventually approved by the American bishops in 1992 and finally accepted by the appropriate Roman office in 1997. The four-volume *Lectionary for Mass*, which we cited earlier, contains those translations for Sundays and Solemnities as well as for weekdays and other celebrations.[35]

People working on the Final English Revision of this second edition of the *Lectionary for Mass* had three goals in mind: maximum fidelity to the biblical text, greater ease in proclamation, and accurate translation of gender-inclusive scriptural terms.

Scripture scholars, language experts, and liturgical leaders struggling to achieve a greater inclusivity emended the base text in over three hundred instances to achieve a more faithful rendering of inclusive words or phrases as they occur in the original Greek or Hebrew text.[36]

The results of their labors, alas, have probably proved disappointing and unsatisfactory to ardent activists on both sides of the controversy. They did not go far enough for those dedicated to inclusive language; they moved too far for those opposed to such inclusivity.

To open up the Bible more fully and lavishly for all worshipers, that new *Lectionary for Mass* contains these components:

Sundays and Feasts. There are three readings for each Mass: the first usually from the Old Testament, the second from writings of the apostles (from a Letter, Acts of the Apostles, or the Book of Revelation), and the third from the Gospel. These texts are arranged according to a three-year cycle. Consequently, we hear the same passage every fourth year. The readings follow a pattern that is either thematic or semicontinuous, depending upon the specific celebration.

Weekdays. The Gospels are arranged in a single year-long series. During the thirty-four weeks of Ordinary

Time, the first readings are arranged in a two-year cycle. Series I is for odd years; Series II is for even years. The Advent, Christmas, Lent, and Easter seasons have special weekday readings.

Celebrations of Saints. For some saints, there are proper readings for their celebrations. For others, there is a wide selection of common readings from which to choose.

Special Masses. The *Lectionary* contains a wealth of texts for use at ritual Masses (like marriages or funerals), votive Masses, and Masses on special occasions. It has become customary for engaged couples to select from the many available options the readings that they find most expressive of their love and hopes. It is also now becoming more common for families to choose biblical passages for the funeral of someone they love.

❖

With the conclusion of the Opening Prayer, the congregation sits down to hear the Word of God. This seated posture expresses and fosters an attitude of receptivity, attentiveness, and respectful listening.

After the introduction of the vernacular into eucharistic celebrations, a spirited debate developed between biblical scholars and liturgical leaders. Should the readings from Scripture be read by the people, or should the people simply listen with full attention as the reader proclaims them? That controversy raised a very practical question: Are the biblical excerpts to be printed in participation aids or deliberately omitted?

Persons on both sides of the debate organized a conference in the Twin Cities some thirty years ago to discuss the issue. Scriptural scholars argued that by reading along with the lector, the members of the gathered community receive the Word of God through two senses: the eyes and the ears, by sight and sound. Liturgical leaders countered that attentive, focused listening links us with a living person whose individual faith during the proclamation adds a dimension that is otherwise missed. If members of the community have their heads down with eyes fixed on the printed page, they barely connect with the lector addressing them.

That Minnesota conference cleared the air and clarified opponents' positions, but did not resolve the matter. Most parishes today provide missalettes, hymnals, or other worship aids that include the scriptural texts; some parishes, espousing the liturgical ideal, provide similar items, but without the biblical excerpts.

After three decades of experience, I can make the following observations: The majority of Catholics at Mass prefer to have the Scripture passages printed and available within their worship aids in case they do wish to read the text. However, a well-trained, dynamic reader will capture the faithful's attention, even if they habitually read along with the lector.

When blind lector Kathy O'Neill makes her way to the ambo in our cathedral on the arm of a companion and guide, places the brown Braille book on the podium, and proclaims the Word as her fingers trace over the raised letters, no one reads from the missalette. Everyone listens.

When bespectacled and diminutive seventh grader Peter Cantone proclaims the Scriptures, doing so as well as any adult lector, no one reads. Everyone listens.

Even in the best of times and the best of parishes, the quality of lectors varies greatly. With at least a few, it is always difficult to hear them or to grasp easily the content of the biblical message that they proclaim. The quality of amplifying systems in churches also varies tremendously. Moreover, every parish has a significant number of people with impaired hearing. That makes essential at least the ready availability of worship aids with biblical passages included. The installation of personalized wireless assistance transistors can be relatively inexpensive. To install such a system and make its presence known through the parish bulletin gives great encouragement to those with impaired hearing and raises the consciousness of others.

FIRST READING

According to our artificial but still helpful "mountain" metaphor describing Mass, God now speaks to us. We can imagine the Father addressing us through the first and second biblical readings. Selections for the first proclamation are generally, but not necessarily, from the Hebrew Scriptures. The second reading, as we will see, is most often from the apostolic letters.[37]

For example, during the Easter season, the first reading is from the Acts of the Apostles arranged in a three-year cycle of parallel and progressive selections. Thus, following celebration at Easter of the Lord's Paschal mystery of dying, rising, and returning, we annually recall and relive for nearly fifty days the life and growth of the early church.[38] At weekday Masses, the initial reading (and the only one before the Gospel) in that two-year cycle may be either an Old or New Testament excerpt.

Three principles govern the selection of these readings: they are to be "semicontinuous," "thematic," and "relational." "Semicontinuous" means that for a period of time we read consecutively from a given book. Thus, during the week we may hear over a number of days excerpts from a particular letter written by St. Paul. Or every third year during the summer we listen to consecutive passages from John's Gospel. The "semi" warns us that we are not covering all verses of every book, nor every book of the Bible, nor each book in order. However, if a person participated in Mass every day for three years, that person would have heard verses from nearly every book in the Bible, with substantial excerpts from some of them.

"Thematic" means that a common element, idea, or message runs through both or all three readings. For example, in the assigned passages for Sundays and weekdays during Advent, Lent, and Easter, a similar theme appears in each of the excerpts.

"Relational" means that frequently we will discover a story, person, or idea that connects especially the first reading and the Gospel. An event or teaching of the New Testament is more or less explicitly linked to the

Old Testament. In fact, developers of the *Lectionary* selected the Old Testament excerpts primarily because of
their relationship to the New Testament, in particular to
the Gospel readings.[39] For example, on Monday of the
Fourth Week of Lent, the Gospel excerpt from John's
first chapter relates the story of the woman caught in
adultery and threatened with death by stoning in accord
with the Mosaic law. Reading I, drawn from Daniel 13,
recounts the similar trials of Susanna, falsely accused of
adultery.

Those who would like to pursue this selection of texts
further or locate where a particular biblical excerpt occurs in the *Lectionary* will find the Index of Readings in
the back of the volume both helpful and fascinating.[40]

THE WORD OF THE LORD

At the conclusion of the first reading the lector, in a
model situation, pauses for a moment, looks intently at
the assembly, and then with a slightly altered and perhaps more definitive tone says: "The Word of the Lord."
That phrase, both a statement and an invitation, origi-
nates from the Latin *Verbum Dei*. In the first years of
use the translation was "This is the Word of the Lord."
Relatively recent directives shortened that conclusion to
"The Word of the Lord."[41]

The phrase reinforces our faith in the inspired nature
of what we have just heard and elicits from us the familiar response of gratitude, "Thanks be to God." While

usually the statement/invitation and response are said, both may be sung, even with someone else singing "The Word of the Lord."

A significant silent pause should follow, allowing the biblical message to reach our hearts. Unfortunately, the more common procedure is to move almost immediately on to the responsorial psalm.

RESPONSORIAL PSALM

St. Benedict once recommended that we listen to Scripture "with the ear of our hearts." This means hearing the words with our ears, allowing them to penetrate our minds, and then accepting them into our hearts. The responsorial psalm follows the first reading and facilitates this "ear of the heart" process. Usually based upon or connected with the initial biblical excerpt, the psalm enables us to respond to God's words with God's word, since these psalm verses also are inspired texts. The psalms convey the deepest sentiments of the human heart — awe and adoration, sadness and remorse, confidence and surrender, joy and gladness.

The 150 psalms are essentially songs, intended, therefore, to be sung. The most common and preferred method for such singing is antiphonal, or responsorial. In this system, the cantor or leader of song chants the verses; the whole community sings the response, or antiphon. However, the psalm may be recited in various ways or read reflectively with an instrumental music background.

To facilitate sung participation, liturgical planners may substitute a common or seasonal psalm in place of the assigned text. A parish, for example, may use only a dozen of these common psalms a year with the hope that the increased frequency will produce a greater familiarity with the antiphon and greater ease in psalm singing.

Songs are not approved replacements for psalms, even though songs are sometimes substituted at parishes in the United States.

Second Reading

On Sundays, solemn feast days, and special occasions God our Father continues to speak to us in a second reading. The semicontinuous concept appears especially in this second reading. There is often a connection between the first reading and the Gospel, but seldom is there a direct link between the second reading and the other two.

The second reading frequently features a "semicontinuous" excerpt from an apostolic letter. For example, on the Sixteenth Sunday of the Year, Cycle C, the first reading and the Gospel both deal with the issues of hospitality and serving an appropriate meal to guests. In Reading I, from Genesis, Abraham and Sarah host three strangers and swiftly prepare food for them. The Gospel, from Luke, recounts the visit of Jesus to the home of Martha and Mary, with Martha busying herself with all the details of hospitality.

Reading II, on the other hand, is an excerpt from the letter of Paul to the Colossians (1:24–28). The reading for the previous Sunday was Colossians 1:15–20; the following two Sundays will excerpt 2:12–14 and 3:1–5, 9–11 from the same letter. Then the *Lectionary* moves on to the letter to the Hebrews.

It is preferable to have separate lectors for each reading. The common practice today also is to have the readers emerge from the community for the proclamation and not remain in the sanctuary for the entire Mass.

ALLELUIA

Liturgical changes since the Second Vatican Council emphasize that all of Sacred Scripture, both Old and New Testaments, is inspired by God and forms a single Word of God. Hence there is only one location for proclamation of the biblical excerpts: the ambo, or lectern.

At the same time, the church dramatizes in various ways the unique dignity of the Gospel words: (1) A deacon or lector carries the separate Book of Gospels, with its richly ornamented binding, in the entrance procession, holding the volume at eye level, and leaves it upright on the altar at the beginning of Mass. (2) The priest or deacon, following a pause after the second reading, and sometimes flanked by candles and incense, transports the Book of Gospels from the altar to the ambo. (3) The priest quietly asks a blessing prior to the Gospel reading with words to this effect: "The Lord be in your heart and on your lips that you may worthily proclaim his Gospel. In the name.... "[42] (4) The priest or deacon may incense the Gospel book just prior to reading the text. (5) Following the Gospel proclamation, the priest or deacon situates the Book of Gospels in a dignified place of honor for the balance of the Mass.

A chanting of Alleluia accompanies the procession with the Gospel book from altar to ambo. This Hebrew word means "Praise God" or "Praise Yahweh." It is intended to be a sung shout of praise and thanksgiving, not because of what has just been heard, but because of what is about to be done: the proclamation of the Gospel. It should heighten our awareness of Christ's presence in the words of Matthew, Mark, Luke, or John.

Because the tone of Alleluia is joyful and triumphant, we omit it during penitential times like Lent. It is preferable for parishes to use only a few different melodies, few enough so that the entire congregation can easily join in the repetitious singing and yet numerous enough so that the repetition does not become monotonous. When the Alleluia is not sung, it is better to omit the word entirely from that part of the Mass.

GOSPEL

When the home batter hits a ball out of the park, the fans almost always leaps to their feet and shout for joy. When our president enters the press room for a media conference, participants immediately cease conversations and rise to greet him. In the first instance, the standing posture denotes victory and jubilation. In the second, it communicates awe and respect. A parallel exists when the assembly rises, sings the Alleluia, and remains standing for the Gospel. Our posture indicates that we rejoice over the good news of Christ's victory for us and reverence the sacred words about to be proclaimed.

Only a priest or deacon proclaims the Gospel. If there is no deacon present, a priest other than the one presiding carries out the proclamation. If neither deacon nor other priest is available, the presiding priest proclaims the sacred text.

The proclaimer greets the people with "The Lord be with you." While announcing the text, "A reading from the holy Gospel according to...," he makes the sign of the cross first on the book, then on his forehead, lips, and breast. Those present make the same gesture and respond, "Glory to you, Lord."[43] This gesture, often curiously made and frequently not understood, denotes our desire to grasp the words of Christ with our minds, speak them with our lips, and believe them with our hearts.

In the mountain metaphor, God continues to speak to us, now with God the Son proclaiming the divine message through the words of Jesus. As we have seen, there are repeated teachings in the church about Christ's presence in the proclamation of the Sacred Scriptures, particularly in the Gospel. At the end of the Gospel proclamation, the proclaimer pauses and then says: "The Gospel of the Lord." The people respond: "Praise to you, Lord Jesus

Christ," in itself a verbalization of their belief that the Savior truly is present in these words.

The Gospel may be sung. Even if the actual text is not chanted, the introductions and conclusion might be sung to facilitate a sung response by the congregation. On solemn occasions, the sung Alleluia might be repeated after the Gospel proclamation.

Following the proclamation and final statement, the proclaimer kisses the book, a gesture of honor, respect, and reverence, and says quietly, "May the words of the Gospel wipe away our sins."[44]

HOMILY

The final element in the downward slope of the mountain occurs in the homily, or sermon, during which God the Holy Spirit speaks to us.

In the early Christian centuries preaching flowed from the texts of the Mass and led to the Liturgy of the Eucharist, which immediately followed. Called a homily, that is, a conversation or address on a religious topic, it formed an integral part of the Mass.

During medieval days, however, the practice of a sermon began to develop, also a religious conversation, speech, or address, but separated, as it were, from the eucharistic liturgy itself. Priests delivered sermons outside of Mass. Moreover, even during the Eucharist there were sometimes prayers, gestures, or places for preaching that further reinforced this separation: for example, a song or prayer to the Holy Spirit for guidance, a dramatic sign of the cross at a sermon's beginning and end, a pulpit quite divorced from the sanctuary and perhaps more dramatic in size than the altar.

The present Mass format restores both the name "homily" and the earlier understanding of this preaching:

- Directives now term inadvisable the practice of beginning and ending the homily with the sign of the cross.

- The homily is strongly recommended, required at certain Masses, and urged at all Eucharists, since "it forms part of the liturgy itself."[45]

- The homily should explain some reading of the Holy Scripture, text of the Mass, mystery of the season, or feast of the day, and apply this message to the needs of the congregation seated before the preacher.[46]

- The preacher may speak from the presidential chair, from the ambo, or from a place that is closer to the congregation if that location will promote more effective communication.

Some years ago a national body of liturgical leaders surveyed Catholics to determine their criteria for evaluating a weekend eucharistic liturgy. Preaching headed the list. The average person, according to that study, judges the quality of a Mass by the quality of the homily.

Most priests I know take their preaching responsibilities very seriously. They work hard at the task and understand the great challenges before them. After all, their audiences, even though captive ones, are extremely diverse. They bring to Mass different backgrounds, different moods, and different expectations.

Priests experience surprising reactions to the words we preach. The homily we thought was outstanding generates no comment at all. Homilies we judged disasters stimulate praise and even acknowledged conversions.

During the last two or three decades, more and more preachers have sought assistance in homily preparation from members of their congregations. The church officially encourages this process today. That shared effort can take many forms but basically involves praying and reflecting together over the texts of the Mass or mystery about to be celebrated, trying to connect human life experiences with the Spirit's divine message.

A dynamic Passionist preacher dropped me a note after I had published an article about this type of lay involvement in homily preparation. "Joe," he wrote, "you are right on target. For a long time, priests have been answering questions no one has been asking!" Through such shared, prayerful preparation, the preacher at least may learn what the real questions are, might discover some answers, and will surely have practical illustrations for his homily.

Despite hard work and careful preparing, homilies can still fall short and leave something to be desired. Our attention may wander and our eyelids droop. But if we listen with open hearts, the Holy Spirit will use a word, a phrase, a concept, a story from the homily to speak to us, to touch us.

PROFESSION OF FAITH

On weekends and major feasts, having heard the Father, Son, and Holy Spirit speak to us through the biblical readings and the homily, after a pause for a few moments of silent reflection upon these inspired words, we rise to express our faith in them. This standing posture mirrors our respectful behavior at the pledge of allegiance before the flag or at the singing of the national anthem. We affirm together the truths of our Catholic tradition.

We constantly express this affirmation through the Nicene Creed, which contains a summary of the major mysteries of Catholicism. In the Mass of 1570, this part of the Mass was known as the "Credo," or "I believe," from the first word of the formula. That individualized format indicates its original function as a profession of faith prior to baptism.

The 1970 Order of Mass has altered that formula slightly, stressing instead the community dimension in this profession of faith by beginning with the plural, "We believe in one God. . . . "[47]

The Nicene identification dates back to the creed's origin at the Council of Nicea (325), although that formula was further adjusted by the Councils of Constantinople (381) and Chalcedon (451). In certain circumstances, the community recites the Apostles' Creed, termed that not because it had been written by the apostles, but because it dates back to the time of the apostles and was the baptismal creed for early Christians.

In either formula, we have a summary of the Catholic Church's major beliefs. It contains, directly, the major truths of Catholicism, but not all of them. For example, there is no mention of the Eucharist in either creedal formula. Nevertheless, all the truths of the Catholic religion are included indirectly or implicitly within the creeds through the final phrase in which we embrace the "holy, catholic, and apostolic church."

The Creed is meant to be recited rather than sung, even though the Gregorian chant "Credo in unum Deum..." would still stir past musical memories of older Catholics.

On some occasions, we follow a question-and-answer format for the Apostles' Creed. When we celebrate baptism or confirmation at Mass, the baptismal profession of faith replaces the creed.

Church rules direct that everyone present make a profound bow at the phrase "by the power of the Holy Spirit he was born of the Virgin Mary, and became man" or, in the new translation, he "was incarnate of the Holy Spirit."[48] The rubrical regulations on this particular point seemingly are seldom observed.

GENERAL INTERCESSIONS

After reciting or singing the Creed, we remain standing for the General Intercessions, or Prayer of the Faithful. The church terms these petitions the "general" intercessions because they are spoken on behalf of widespread and diverse people and situations both at home and abroad, both in the local church and the universal church. The church calls them the prayers of the "faithful" because they come from the hearts and lips of believers who, having heard God's Word, now respond with intercessions or petitions for others, especially those outside or beyond the assembly gathered for worship.

The practice and format dates back to the earliest Christian tradition. We see vestiges of that tradition annually during the Good Friday service. In those ten General Intercessions the community prays for the church, the pope, the clergy and laity of the church, those preparing for baptism, the unity of Christians, the Jewish people, those who do not believe in Christ, those who do not believe in God, all in public office, and those in special need.[49]

As a regular part of Sunday Mass the General Intercessions disappeared around the sixth century. However, at the Second Vatican Council, the bishops directed that the "common prayer," or "Prayer of the Faithful," be restored after the Gospel and homily, particularly on Sundays and holy days of obligation. They also specified, although in a generic way, the beneficiaries of these petitions: the church, civil authorities, people oppressed by various needs, all humankind, and the salvation of the entire world. That list looks for its basis to Paul's words to Timothy (1 Tim. 2:1–2).[50]

Today's Mass carries out this mandate and lists the customary intentions: the needs of the church, of those burdened with any trouble, of civil authorities, of the whole world, and of the local community.

This Prayer of the Faithful has now become a standard part of Catholic Masses, including liturgies in which the intercessions are not expressly required, such as weekday, baptismal, wedding, and funeral Masses.

The presiding priest introduces the General Intercessions, inviting the assembly to participate. The petitions are proposed by a deacon, another minister, or even members of the congregation; they do so at the ambo or another suitable location. The petitions may be recited or sung, with the people's response either silence, a standard common phrase (e.g., "Lord, receive our prayer"), or responsive petitions that vary from time to time.

The intercessions themselves should be brief, clear, and easily understood. Many parishes employ books or published materials that provide ready-made prayers of the faithful. They are usually liturgically correct and doctrinally sound, expressed in carefully crafted language. However, producers have necessarily prepared these texts months in advance. They lack, therefore, both a local and immediate quality to them.

Some of us recommend that those responsible for the General Intercessions compose them on Saturday morning. While they may build upon the petitions contained in those commercial publications, these individuals would want to check the morning paper and media news for perhaps two events that will be on everyone's mind over the weekend. In addition, they could have one petition that reflects the preacher's homily.

In this fashion, when people leave Mass and arrive at home, they will find several topics of great concern mentioned in the General Intercessions carried on the paper's front page or discussed over the television news. However, current critical events will never find their way into the weekend's worship if the liturgical planners rely totally upon previously prepared prayers of the faithful.

Most parishes include explicit mention of individuals who are sick or deceased. In my current and previous assignments, I have found that powerfully effective. However, the list of ill persons quickly grows, soon reaching an unwieldy number. We have resolved that dilemma by printing the entire list (our last one had 775 names on it) as an insert in the bulletin every six weeks. In addition, we post these names on the major announcement boards.

Moreover, on the weekend the full list appears, we take about five minutes at the end of the petitions for a unique "prayer for the sick" experience. The assembly sits for this period. The priest reads about a dozen names and concludes, "Let us pray for these who are ill." The people respond: "Lord, heal them." On subsequent weekends we mention only new names added since the list appeared. Then, six weeks later we update the list and begin the process again.

This note from a young man in his late twenties testifies to the positive impact these prayers of the faithful can have for a family or person struggling with a serious illness:

In September 1997 I asked that my sister, Mary Kay Donnelly, be added to the cathedral's weekly prayer list for those in need. At that time, my sister had been recently diagnosed with advanced breast cancer. The outlook for her recovery was not good. During the following months she endured chemotherapy and radiation treatments and even underwent a bone marrow transplant. It was a difficult and trying time for my sister especially but also for the rest of my family. Knowing that the members of the cathedral family were remembering my sister in their prayers was of great comfort.

I am pleased to inform you that my sister has been classified as cancer free. Her outlook is good and her spirits have rebounded. Please remove her name from the prayer list. My heartfelt thanks to you and all of those who included Mary Kay in their prayers. My sister's recovery is a wonderful reminder of God's love for all of us and the true power of prayer.

The author admits that he previously had grumbled about praying for the long list of sick people, but when cancer attacked his forty-two-year-old sister, that attitude changed drastically, as his letter indicates. The prayers of the faithful are indeed powerful in many ways.

We have spoken to God, and in response to our words God has spoken to us, Father, Son, and Holy Spirit. Now that we have traveled over this first mountain, the action moves from the ambo to the altar.

CHAPTER SIX

LITURGY OF THE EUCHARIST

*The Last Supper, in which Christ instituted the
memorial of his death and resurrection, is made
continuously present in the church when the priest,
representing Christ the Lord, does the same thing
which the Lord himself did and committed to the
disciples to do in memory of him, instituting the
paschal sacrifice and meal.*[51]

The Eucharist as mystery includes three notions: sacrifice,
sacrament, and Presence.

The Mass is a sacrificial action, the re-presenting of
what Christ did on Holy Thursday, Good Friday, and
Easter Sunday, as well as public worship of the Father
through the Son in the Holy Spirit. It is, therefore, the
"paschal sacrifice."

The Eucharist, however, is at the same time a sacred banquet, a holy feast, a rite of eating and drinking the body and blood of Christ in Communion. It is, therefore, "the paschal . . . meal."

The Presence of Christ reserved in the tabernacle for later use with the sick or for personal adoration depends upon the Eucharistic Sacrifice, or Mass, for its existence. Jesus became present through this sacrificial action under the signs of bread and wine, later to be consumed in Communion or adored within the tabernacle.

The locale of the Mass now moves from the ambo (the table of God's Word) to the altar of this sacrifice/banquet (the table of the body of Christ, or table of the Lord).[52] We embark upon the second and larger mountain of the Mass. In the Liturgy of the Eucharist we will give (not speak) to God and, in response, God gives (not speaks) to us.

On the upward slope we present the needed ritual elements (bread, water, and wine). We also give our financial donations for the church and the poor. Finally, symbolized through these items, we offer our very lives — all we are, possess, and have done during the past week.

The priest transforms our gifts into Christ himself at the consecration, or institution narrative. He, with us, subsequently offers these most precious gifts, the body and blood of Jesus, to the Father. Quite remarkably, we are, therefore, able to give, as it were, God to God.

The Our Father, or Lord's Prayer, begins the downward slope as God responds to our gifts by giving Christ to us in Communion.

PREPARATION OF THE GIFTS

PREPARATION OF THE ALTAR

The assembly sits after the General Intercessions, or Prayer of the Faithful, as the gifts and altar are prepared. To indicate the shift in focus, some parishes move lighted candles from near the ambo to beside the altar. Others have large, fixed candles positioned by the altar, which have remained unlit for the Liturgy of the Word; servers approach and light them for the forthcoming Liturgy of the Eucharist.

The altar itself ideally is kept free of everything during the service of the Word, with the frequent exception of a large cloth that drapes down on two or four sides of the altar.

While ushers gather the collection of money, servers or sometimes other members of the congregation bring needed items to the altar. These include:

Corporal. This square, white, folded linen cloth takes its name from the Latin word *corpus,* which means "body." The consecrated body and blood of Christ will soon rest upon this corporal, thus the name given to that unique cloth. The corporal usually has a cross woven into its center. It has been ironed and folded in such a way that the cloth forms nine squares. In former days of intense religious symbolism, some viewed this as another image of the Trinity with the multiplication of threes and the one cloth. The servers unfold the corporal and place it at the center of the altar near the edge at which the presiding priest will stand. It should be large enough to accommodate all the vessels that will be brought to the altar.

Purificator. This is another white linen cloth often marked with a cross and carefully folded. As the name suggests, it is used to purify the sacred vessels, particularly the chalice.

Chalice. The chalice contains the wine mixed with water, ultimately to be transformed into the Precious Blood of Christ. Thus chalices should be made of worthy and durable materials. Traditionally these were fashioned of gold or silver with pertinent symbols or words engraved on their surfaces. In recent years, ceramic, wood, and even glass chalices have appeared — the last with the advantage of making the wine more visible.

Missal or, more accurately, Sacramentary. Instead of one liturgical book, the *Roman Missal,* today's Mass has two volumes, the *Lectionary* of Scripture readings and the *Sacramentary* of prayers and rubrics. The "rubrics" are rules governing liturgical actions, for example, "the priest genuflects" or "the priest extends his hands." They are termed rubrics from the Latin root meaning "red," because these directives are printed in red. Those preparing the altar place the *Sacramentary* in the center, but a bit away from the edge where the priest stands.

COLLECTION

The priest remains seated as people prepare the altar and ushers take up the collection. In the early Christian centuries, the congregation brought forward real gifts more often than legal tender. Designated persons carried to the altar the bread, wine, and water as well as foodstuffs and other items for the poor. Over time these processions disappeared. Our current Mass restores the practice. It suggests that members of the congregation carry forward the bread and wine required as well as other gifts for the needs of the church and the poor.[53] The priest or deacon receiving these items places the eucharistic elements on the altar and the other gifts near, but not on, the altar. In a few American churches the entire congregation walks to the sanctuary and deposits individual gifts in receptacles near the altar.

Those who actively promote stewardship offer a few practical suggestions to underscore the importance and meaning of the collection or gathering process:

• There should be a sufficient number of ushers, female and male, to facilitate a swift gathering of the financial gifts.

• Baskets that can be passed from person to person should be used rather than long-handled receptacles maneuvered by the ushers.

• Envelopes are appropriate gift wrappers for the money offering.

• Special envelopes for children can provide a space for them to note their weekly time and talent offering for others, as well as their treasure gift.

- A large, open, dignified basket or other receptacle can be carried by a member of the congregation and presented to the priest, who then places it before the altar in full view of the people for the rest of the Mass.

- Instrumental or choral background music during the collection is more appropriate than congregational singing. (It is difficult simultaneously to take out one's offering, pass the basket, open up a music book, and sing.)

- The presiding priest who places his own envelope into the basket at the proper time encourages others by his example.

- Careful selection of gift bearers insures that an inclusive and significant number of parishioners over a period of time will have the experience of presenting the gifts.

- When churches encourage a food donation weekend on a regular basis, placing the bags and cartons of food around the altar can powerfully symbolize a parish's commitment to the poor.

BLESSING

Prior to 1970, the preparing of the altar with accompanying prayers was called and understood as the offertory. We presented the gifts and ourselves; the priest offered them to God. The texts, recited silently by the celebrant and frequently read in translation by the people, contained that notion. Vatican Council II altered the approach to this part of the Mass. Some elements (e.g., the washing of hands) were retained but adjusted; others were replaced (e.g., the offering formulas by Jewish table blessing prayers).

The notion of bringing ourselves, symbolized by our gifts, to the altar for offering and consecration to God is still appropriate. However, the emphasis now shifts to this action as a simple preparation of our gifts, which will be transformed by the Eucharistic Prayer, and then these gifts, absorbed as it were into Christ, are offered to the Father. The real, true, and best offering occurs, therefore, after the institution narrative and prior to the Our Father.

Instead of offering the bread and wine, the priest lifts first the bread and then the cup just slightly above the altar and speaks aloud, if there is no music, or inaudibly, if there is, a prayer that "blesses" God. The notion of "blessing" God may seem foreign to English-speaking worshipers. "To praise" God conveys the notion intended here.

These formularies originate in our Jewish roots. We praise God for everything in creation, including the human talents that can transform crushed wheat and pressed grapes into bread and wine. "Blessed are you, Lord, God of all creation."

Jesus, Mary, and Joseph, as faithful orthodox Jews, presumably followed a tradition that urged believers to utter a blessing of God over a hundred times each day. They blessed or praised God for everything from a gorgeous sunset to a gentle breeze.

When there is no music and the priest recites aloud the two "blessed" formularies, the people respond with a similar acclamation or prayer of praise, "Blessed be God forever."[54]

Parish liturgical committees seek to use the type and quantity of bread and wine that will be visible to and sufficient for the community assembled for a particular Mass. They will, ideally, eat and drink elements presented and consecrated at this Eucharist, not carried over from a previous Mass. Church regulations for many decades have strongly and repeatedly urged this point; implementation of the goal has been a challenge and unevenly executed in the United States.

MIXING THE WINE AND WATER

Before elevating the cup a little and blessing God for the gift of wine, the priest (or deacon) pours a few drops of water into the chalice or flagon of wine. As he does this, the priest (or deacon) says quietly:

> By the mystery of this water and wine may we come to share in the divinity of Christ, who humbled himself to share in our humanity.[55]

Because of the distance from the altar and the quiet, almost silent recitation of those words, most members of the assembly may hardly notice and certainly not understand the significance of this highly symbolic action. It has a long and diverse history. An ancient rule, originating in Greece but practiced in Palestine during Christ's time, required that some water must be mingled with the wine. We find writings in the second century that mention this practice. That addition would naturally temper the wine. Over subsequent centuries the mingling by which the wine and water became inseparable took on a variety of symbolic meanings. This gesture thus came to symbolize among other truths:

- the union of divine and human elements in Christ;

- the descent of God's Son into this world, becoming one of us;

- the close bond between Christ and his church;

- the elevation of Christians, through baptism, to a sharing by grace of Jesus' divine nature;

- the pouring out of blood and water from the Savior's side on the cross;

- the intimate union of Christ and ourselves.[56]

The mixing of water with wine is a minor action, but one that can symbolize many truths of the faith.

When there are several cups, the water is poured into only one. It is not necessary to add a drop of water to each wine receptacle, although some might dispute that statement. This issue can easily be resolved on the parish level. Usually one large flagon will suffice for a Mass. The priest or deacon can pour the drops of water into that flagon and recite the prayer. Then he pours the appropriate amount into the cup or chalice that will be used during the institution narrative.

INCENSATION

During the middle of the twentieth century some referred to Catholic churches as places of "bells and smells." They meant that servers frequently rang little bells during worship services and that the aroma of incense often filled the air. Those experiences are less common now as we move from one millennium to another. Few parishes continue to have altar servers ring special bells at Mass. Incense is seldom used at Sunday Masses and is reserved for funerals and special devotional events.

There were no church restrictions or prohibitions that caused this decline, only a combination of complex factors. Ironically, while bells and incense generally disappeared in Catholic liturgies, those two elements, especially the latter, grew in popularity in the secular American culture, particularly among young people.

The 1970 Mass directives still provide opportunities for the use of incense, with the preparation of gifts a major occasion for that action. There are two basic meanings to this gesture. First, those gently rising clouds of incense symbolize the church's offering and our prayer rising to the sight of God. Both Old and New Testament biblical texts mention this practice and metaphor in worship services (Ps. 141:2; Rev. 8:4). Second, the gesture honors the object or persons being incensed. It recognizes the dignity (through creation and baptism) of each as well as the special presence of Christ in the priest celebrant, the ministers, and the rest of the assembly. The earlier Mass contained precise directions and accompanying words for the incensation of gifts and altar. Those have been omitted from the present missal. We continue to incense altar and gifts as we did in the past, but simply with natural movements that reflect the symbolic meaning of the action.[57]

Roman Catholics and visitors to our services most often experience the use of incense at funerals. Incensation is a more definitive part of the burial liturgy and includes incensing the cross, Easter candle, and casket. For this action to accomplish its purpose, there needs to be sufficient burning charcoal and incense to produce visible clouds emerging from the incensation vessel (called a thurible).

The priest walks around the casket and incenses the body enclosed within it. This symbol dramatizes our faith, which teaches that the remains of the deceased, originally given life by God, formed a temple for the Holy Spirit while on earth and will be raised up on the last day. They deserve our honor and respect.

WASHING OF THE HANDS

Prior to and after the incensation, the priest performs two gestures and recites quietly accompanying phrases expressing humility, contrition, and the desire for a purified heart: (1) He bows from the waist and recites a brief prayer taken from one of the oldest formularies of the *Roman Missal;* based on Daniel 3:39, it begs God to receive and be pleased with the sacrifice that we offer "with humble and contrite hearts."[58] (2) He moves to the side and washes his hands.

In early Christian centuries the congregation brought not only bread, wine, and money, but food and other gifts for the church and poor. The priest, after handling those gifts, understandably needed to cleanse his hands. That necessity no longer exists today, but the symbolic gesture, which has its roots in Jewish as well as early Christian traditions, continues to have value. We express our desire and need for inner purity as we begin this sacred and holy action. To achieve its full value, this symbolic gesture requires a deliberate action and the use of an easily visible pitcher, basin, and towel, and an abundant supply of water. Both hands, not a few fingers, need washing in full view of the assembly.

At this point during the earlier Mass, the priest, still inaudibly, recited an entire psalm. The current Mass simplifies that action by providing one verse only from Psalm 51: "Lord, wash away my iniquity; cleanse me from my sin."[59]

PRAYER OVER THE GIFTS

During the Mass there are three prayers that have a parallel purpose: The Opening Prayer concludes the Introductory Rites; the Prayer over the Gifts concludes the preparation of these elements; the Prayer after Communion concludes the Communion ritual.

In the previous Mass celebrated in the United States, the Prayer over the Gifts was popularly called the "Secret." It gained that title because the priest recited this text in a hushed voice. The conclusion, however, *Per omnia saecula saeculorum,* was recited or sung aloud and actually formed part of the introduction to the preface.

The present Mass makes modest but important modifications in this prayer:

- It is now termed the Prayer over the Gifts, which the priest says or sings aloud.

- It concludes the preparation of the gifts and elicits a response, "Amen," from the people.

- While the prayer does point forward to the Eucharistic Prayer, it is more of a conclusion to the preparation of gifts.

- The priest should pause long enough before continuing to indicate an end to the preparation of gifts and the start of a new section of Mass, the Eucharistic Prayer.

- While the conclusion to the Opening Prayer uses a full Trinitarian formula, the Prayers over the Gifts and after Communion use the short formula "through Christ our Lord" or "in the name of Jesus the Lord."

- An option proposed by the American bishops allows the priest to use the traditional formula "Pray, that our sacrifice may be acceptable . . . " or simply to invite the people to prayer with "Let us pray."[60]

The preparation of the altar and gifts, while rich in symbolism, nevertheless should be relatively simple. It concludes with the section's most important prayer, the Prayer over the Gifts.

EUCHARISTIC PRAYER

We continue our ascent of the second and larger mountain of the Mass, our giving to God. Having presented the gifts and prepared the altar, we now join in the transformation of these items and ourselves into Christ and in the offering of Jesus to the Father in the Holy Spirit.

This section, the heart, center, and climax of the entire celebration, also highlights the thanksgiving motif of the Mass and why we often call it a "Eucharist," or "Eucharistic Celebration." The Greek word *eucharistia,* from which "Eucharist" is derived, means thanksgiving. The introductory dialogue makes the theme explicit: "Let us give thanks to the Lord our God." "It is right to give him thanks and praise."[61]

The thanksgiving theme emerges again during the narration of the institution. Based on the New Testament accounts of the Last Supper (Matt. 26:26–30; Mark 14:22–26; Luke 22:14–20; 1 Cor. 11:23–26), the Eucharistic Prayer always notes and repeats Jesus' thanksgiving actions and words. For example, "He took bread and gave thanks.... He took the cup. Again he gave you thanks and praise...."[62]

There are profound spiritual realities connected with this essential element of the Eucharist:

- We praise and thank God for all of creation and for saving us.

- Through the power of the Holy Spirit, the body and blood of Christ become present on the altar.

- The people assembled are linked to Christ in offering his memorial sacrifice to the Father.

- We recall Jesus' birth, life, death, and resurrection.

- We re-present and re-live the Last Supper.

- The priest in our name invokes the power of the Holy Spirit upon the gifts, asking that they be sanctified and transformed, and upon all present, that they too be sanctified and transformed, united into the one body of Christ.

- We pray for the living and the dead, seeking to be one with all, a community of persons whose lives reflect love, service, and praise to the glory of God the Father.

The Eucharistic Prayer is fundamentally a dialogue involving the presiding priest and the assembled people. Singing of certain parts facilitates that dialogue and enhances the solemnity of this sacred action.

Each of the Eucharistic Prayers includes the following elements, although their presence is more obvious in some than in others:

- giving thanks, expressed especially in the preface;

- acclamation ("Holy, holy, holy Lord . . . ," or Sanctus);

- Epiclesis, or invocation of the Holy Spirit;

- institution narrative, the recounting and re-presentation of the Last Supper;

- anamnesis, or remembrance, or memorial;

- offering of the spotless Victim Christ and the assembled people with him;

- intercessions for the living and the deceased;

- final doxology in which priest and people give all glory and honor to the almighty Father forever and ever.

Preface

In the Roman Catholic Church there are two major liturgical traditions — Eastern and Western.

The Eastern, or Oriental, tradition links inseparably the introductory preface and prayer proper. That tradition possesses nearly a hundred of these Eucharistic Prayers, with each centering upon a theme, season, mystery, or feast. The presiding priest and people select the Eucharistic Prayer that best fits the occasion.

The Western, or Roman, tradition, on the other hand, uses a variable preface to express the celebration's theme, season, mystery, or feast. Moreover, traditionally there was only one Eucharistic Prayer following the preface, and now there are only a few. The 1570 *Roman Missal,* for example, contained but one Eucharistic Prayer, the "Roman Canon," yet many prefaces.

The 1970 Mass blends and expands upon these two traditions. It has increased the number of prefaces so that currently we may choose from over eighty such formularies. Furthermore, it has developed a Eucharistic Prayer (IV), which, as in the Eastern tradition, links inseparably the preface and the prayer itself.

This Mass also includes additional Eucharistic Prayers for greater variety. Today in the United States priests and liturgy planning committees may select from Eucharistic Prayers I–IV (the principal ones for use throughout the year), from two Reconciliation Eucharistic Prayers, from three for Masses with Children, and from four Eucharistic Prayers for Masses for Various Needs and Occasions, originally approved at a synod in Switzerland. Unfortunately, in too many parishes in the United States, priests have failed to take advantage of this rich variety of alternatives and have often limited themselves to one or two of the approved Eucharistic Prayers. Such a restricted approach minimizes the possibility of freshness and increases the possibility of monotony.

The preface is not an introduction, but the first part of the Eucharistic Prayer, a proclamation establishing the theme for the prayers that follow. It is most appropriately sung and should lead easily and naturally to the people's response in the Sanctus Acclamation.

HOLY, HOLY, HOLY LORD

The people's sung response to the preface, called the Sanctus Acclamation, from the Latin word familiar to many, takes its inspiration from the prophet Isaiah. The prophet saw the Lord seated on a high and lofty throne in the temple surrounded by angels, called seraphim, who cried to one another, "Holy, holy, holy is the LORD of hosts. . . . All the earth is filled with his glory" (Isa. 6:1–4). Some would see in this threefold repetition of "holy" an allusion to the Most Holy Trinity.

This ideally is the people's sung response, or rather the response of both the priest and people chanting together. Therefore, choral renditions that make such congregational participation impossible are inappropriate.

After singing the Sanctus Acclamation, the priest remains standing at the altar to proclaim the prayer. The congregation, according to directives for the United States, kneel from that point until the conclusion of the doxology before the Our Father.

The current Mass norms urge a uniformity in gestures and postures among the assembly at Mass. They also empower bishops to establish specific regulations appropriate for the local situation.[63] The *Roman Missal* specifies that the people kneel at the consecration unless prohibited from doing so because of lack of space, the crowd, or "other reasonable causes."

In our Christian tradition, kneeling can signify various interior attitudes: submission before the Lord; recognition that we are only creatures, who kneel before the Creator; repentance for sin; adoration of an awesome God; humility; a sense of reverence in the presence of the sacred.

The priest prays in the name of the assembly before him, generally with hands outstretched and in a standing position, mirroring the posture described for the Opening Prayer.

INVOCATION OF THE HOLY SPIRIT

The priest, after the Sanctus and before the consecration, extends both hands over the chalice and paten, reciting the required words.

Those words, which vary slightly according to the Eucharistic Prayer, call upon the Father to send the Holy Spirit upon the gifts of bread and wine "that they may become for us the body and blood of our Lord, Jesus Christ." The priest makes the sign of the cross over the offerings as he pronounces these words.[64]

The gesture and the words evoke a variety of memories and meanings. Most Catholics recall experiences in which a priest blessed objects or persons by making the sign of the cross over them. Regular readers of the Bible know how often the laying on of hands effected healing, the coming of the Holy Spirit, or the setting aside and designation of certain persons for special sacred tasks. In Luke 4:40, Jesus "laid his hands on each of them and cured them." In Acts 9:17, Saul, soon to become Paul after his conversion, makes his way to the home of the Christian Ananias. Laying hands on Paul, Ananias said, "The Lord has sent me...that you may regain your sight and be filled with the holy Spirit." In Acts 13:1–3, several early followers of Christ were worshiping the Lord and fasting. While doing so they heard the Holy Spirit direct them to set apart Barnabas and Saul for the work to which God had called them. In response, "completing their fasting and prayer, they laid hands on them and sent them off."

Many of our sacramental rituals, such as confirmation, reconciliation, anointing of the sick, and ordination, include this laying on of hands. These actions convey directly or indirectly, explicitly or implicitly, blessing and healing, forgiveness and consecration, the wisdom and power of the Holy Spirit. Following Sacred Scripture, we image the Holy Spirit as the power moving over the waters to create life at creation and as the power overshadowing Mary to create the child within her.

In the Jewish tradition, the priest on a special day of repentance laid hands upon an animal, the "scapegoat," symbolizing the transmission of all sins to this creature. He then sent the scapegoat out into the desert, into oblivion, thus removing the people's transgressions and casting them into forgetfulness. The connection of this scapegoat with Christ, the Lamb of God, the victim whose sacrificial gift on the cross makes forgiveness and forgetfulness of our sins possible, is clear.

In the current Mass, this invocation (called "epiclesis," a Greek word that means summoning or calling forth) occurs before and after the institution narrative, or consecration. The priest invokes the Holy Spirit, asking the Spirit to transform the bread and wine into Christ's body and blood and to unite all those who receive the consecrated elements into one body, bonded by faith and love. Both the words and gesture should be accomplished with a seriousness and deliberate care to underscore the importance of the moment.

The *Roman Missal* specifically notes that a minister or server may (not must) ring a bell just before the consecration as a signal to the people and also may do so at the showing, or elevation, of the eucharistic bread and the cup.[65] That practice, formerly universal, has now become a minority experience.

NARRATIVE OF THE INSTITUTION AND CONSECRATION OF THE ELEMENTS

The entire Eucharistic Prayer is one unified, continuous action of prayer and praise. It should, therefore, have a certain steady flow from the beginning until the great Amen. On the other hand, the recitation or singing of the Last Supper account sums up what the Mass is about: making present the person of the crucified and risen Lord. Church directives attempt to blend the specialness of the

narrative and consecration with the uninterrupted flow
of the entire Eucharistic Prayer:

- A close look at the *Sacramentary* will reveal that
  the actual consecrating phrases, "Take this, all of
  you, and eat.... Take this, all of you, and drink
  from it... in memory of me," are printed in slightly
  larger type.

- A rubric reminds the priest that these "words of the
  Lord" should be spoken "clearly and distinctly" as
  their meaning dictates.

- The priest is to bow "slightly," not profoundly or
  in exaggerated fashion, as he pronounces the Lord's
  words of consecration.

- After the consecration, the priest shows the blessed
  bread and chalice with blessed wine, doing this with
  deliberation and reverence in such fashion that all can
  see the body and blood of Christ. However, the level
  of elevation should be less than the elevation at the
  conclusion of the Eucharistic Prayer. Moreover, the
  pace of the gesture should not be so pronounced that
  it interrupts the overall movement of the Eucharistic
  Prayer.[66]

Clearly the priest will need to maintain a certain balance
if he wishes to preserve that harmony between the overall
flow of the Eucharistic Prayer and the special significance
of this consecration.

The fact that they actually pronounce Jesus' words of
consecration and bring about the transformation desired

can be a sobering, inspirational reminder to all priest presiders.

GENUFLECTIONS

The earlier Mass required multiple signs of the cross and genuflections. The Second Vatican Council directed planners of the new Mass to change that. The rites, they wrote, should "radiate a noble simplicity," "be short, clear, and free from useless repetition." Moreover, "duplications made with the passage of time are to be omitted as are less useful additions."[67]

The New Order of Mass reflects these directives. It requires now only three signs of the cross: at the beginning and end of Mass and over the gifts at the epiclesis (with an additional sign of the cross in Eucharistic Prayer I). It also reduces the priest's genuflections to only three: after the consecration of the bread and the wine and before receiving Communion.

A genuflection, meaning to bend one's knees, is made by touching the right knee to the ground beside the left foot. It is meant to express with our body an inner attitude of adoration before our God. Some view this as a vestige of medieval days — genuflecting before a secular ruler — and prefer therefore a profound bow instead of a genuflection. Those with arthritis or other ailments that make genuflections burdensome surely welcome that.

MEMORIAL ACCLAMATION

In the Eastern Catholic tradition, the community frequently interrupts the proclamation of the Eucharistic Prayer with acclamations. *The New Order of Mass* injects some of that practice into all the Eucharistic Prayers. There are, of course, the congregationally sung "Holy, holy, holy Lord" and great "Amen." But the 1970 Mass adds the Memorial Acclamation immediately after the consecration.

The priest or deacon invites the people to express their belief in the central mystery of our faith through this response of remembrance, intended to be sung. The congregation then responds with one of four acclamations, sentences that can be rendered in various musical settings.

The "mystery of faith" is reflected in those core truths of the Christian tradition: the paschal mystery of Jesus' entrance into this world, his death, his rising, his coming again, and his presence among us.

This is the first of several Memorial Acclamations contained in the *Order of Mass:*

Priest: Let us proclaim the mystery of faith.

People: Christ has died, Christ is risen, Christ will come again.

REMEMBERING AND OFFERING

We mentioned earlier that the essential offering at Mass occurs not during the Preparation of Gifts, but after the consecration of the elements. A brief prayer to the Father after the memorial acclamation achieves that purpose. It has two major thrusts: remembering and offering.

The aspect of remembering earns this prayer the name "anamnesis," a Greek word that means "remembrance" or "calling to mind." We call to mind, we remember, we carry out this action as a memorial, in memory of the Last Supper, as a faithful fulfillment of his command, "Do this in memory of me" (Luke 22:19). That remembering also recalls all of God's gifts and blessings from the past, which gives us hope for the present and future.

The offering is expressed by the priest speaking in our name and with the entire church, but especially with those gathered here and now, offering in thanks this "holy and living sacrifice" of Christ to the Father in the Holy Spirit. We give to God a most precious gift.

INTERCESSIONS

While still in this sacred, powerful, and special moment, the priest in the people's name calls upon those in heaven, the saints, to speak on our behalf. He always mentions Mary, the Mother of God, and, according to the Eucharistic Prayer, also adds other saints of the church. In Eucharistic Prayer I, the intercessions occur before and after the consecration. Proposed revisions encourage priests to select both male and female saints when using Eucharistic Prayer I.

These petitionary phrases on behalf of the living explicitly mention our Holy Father, the pope; the local bishop(s); the clergy; the laity; and in particular those gathered for this Mass. The intercessions for the deceased are generic, but a formula for an individual person is provided in Masses for the dead.

Doxology

Our ascending slope of giving to God reaches its climax at this concluding action of the Eucharistic Prayer. We call this the doxology, meaning the giving of praise and glory. The priest holds high a container with the consecrated bread in one hand and a cup with the consecrated wine in the other (or the deacon may hold the cup). He sings or at least speaks loudly the familiar formula: "Through him, with him, in him, in the unity of the Holy Spirit, all glory and honor is yours, almighty Father, forever and ever."[68] The people respond with a clear and loud "Amen," the Hebrew word of assent and affirmation.

Church directives encourage creative musical settings that can facilitate a strong "Amen" to the doxology.

The pause that the priest makes following the doxology as well as the change of posture from kneeling to standing emphasize two points: that we have reached the summit of the ascending slope "giving thanks," and we that have begun to descend the slope of God giving to us the Son, Jesus Christ, in Communion.

COMMUNION RITE

THE LORD'S PRAYER

The Our Father serves as an excellent transition and preparation prayer. As a transition, the petitions of its first half move toward God, continuing the thrust of the Eucharistic Prayer. The petitions of its second half move toward the congregation, "Give, forgive, lead, deliver us," establishing the basic direction of the Communion Rite.

As a preparation formulary, its mention of "daily bread" turns our minds and hearts to the eucharistic nourishment we will soon eat and drink. Communion rituals both within and outside Mass developed since the Second Vatican Council always include the Our Father for that very reason.

The general public often distinguishes between the Catholic and Protestant Lord's Prayer. That latter and longer version includes the doxology "For thine is the kingdom...." Scholars today understand that this beautiful phrase was appended to some of the earliest liturgical texts and to the New Testament itself. Strictly speaking, however, those were neither the words of Christ nor an inspired biblical text. Today's Mass resolves the question by blending the two versions. The "Catholic" Our Father begins the section. An expansion or extension of its last petition, called the "embolism," follows: "Deliver us Lord, from every evil...." A doxology, "For the kingdom, the power and the glory are yours now and forever," obviously based on the so-called Protestant ending, concludes this part.

When the Our Father is sung everyone should sing together. The priest sings or says the embolism with the congregation responding by singing or saying the doxology, "For the kingdom.... "[69] Possible revisions suggest that the people may extend their hands apart and upward, the "orans" gesture used by the priest during the Lord's Prayer.

The Our Father also serves as a preparation for what follows. A petition for forgiveness leads into the sign of peace, the gesture of reconciliation. Both remind us that we who are one in the church need to be truly one in heart with each other before receiving the one body and blood of Christ.

SIGN OF PEACE

The introduction or, more accurately, the reintroduction of the sign of peace into the Mass generated perhaps more opposition and controversy than any of the other changes in the liturgy after the Second Vatican Council.

However, the sign of peace was hardly a modern creation. We read about a ritual kiss of peace in the earliest Christian writings and in the sacred Scriptures: St. Paul, for example, urged the Romans to "greet one another with a holy kiss" (Rom. 16:16).

In its first eucharistic manifestation, the sign of peace occurred after the Liturgy of the Word and before presentation of the gifts. The gesture had a double purpose: to affirm the message just spoken and to insure that hearts were one before worshipers brought forth their offerings.

This second goal represented an effort to observe Jesus' teaching about reconciliation in Matthew's Gospel: "If you bring your gift to the altar, and there recall that your brother has anything against you, leave your gift there at the altar, go first and be reconciled with your brother, and then come and offer your gift" (Matt. 5:23–24).

Very soon, however, the sign of peace moved to its present location, after the Lord's Prayer and before Communion. It is no longer a greeting or a welcome, but rather a sign and vehicle of reconciliation. The action looks back to the concluding words of the Our Father — "forgive us as we forgive others" and forward to Communion, reminding us that we must be one with each other in our hearts before daring to become one with each other through receiving the same body and blood of Christ.

The church in the United States leaves the words or gesture by which we implement the sign of peace quite optional. Whatever the gesture — kiss or bow, handshake or hug — the usual accompanying phrase includes the greeting: "Peace." "Peace," *pax* in Latin, mirrors its Jewish companion, *Shalom*. That concept conveys not just the absence of conflict or hostility, but all of God's blessings, total well-being, a life at one with God, others, and creation.

The gesture should generally be horizontal, that is, worshipers sharing the greeting with one another, not vertical, that is, the priest bringing peace from the altar down to the people. Christ is present and active in the community and in each member of the worshiping group. That presence both inspires and can accomplish the reconciliation or harmony sought at this point in the Mass.

Breaking of Bread

The Acts of the Apostles, in the second and fourth chapters, presents an idyllic description of the early Christian communities. They were "of one heart and mind" and devoted themselves "to the breaking of the bread and to the prayers" (Acts 2:42–47; 4:32–35). People at that time often used the term "the breaking of the bread" to describe the Eucharist or the Mass itself. The phrase also denotes the rich and necessary ritual action that follows the sign of peace and precedes Communion.

A powerful intercessory acclamation accompanies the breaking up of the consecrated bread and the pouring of the consecrated wine. The Lamb of God, or Agnus Dei, sung or recited, continues as long as required for the breaking of the bread, or *fractio panis*. The same invocation may be repeated over and over with the response "have mercy on us" until near completion of the breaking and pouring. The final response is always, "grant us peace."[70] Different invocations of Christ may also be inserted into the acclamation.

Some view this last response as connected with the preceding sign of peace and another reminder that Christians should be one in mind and heart prior to receiving the Risen Lord in the Holy Communion.

The word "mercy" means more than our customary English "forgiveness" or "compassion." It embraces all of God's blessings, gifts that we plead for throughout this intercessory acclamation.

The acclamations call upon the Risen Christ before us on the altar, Jesus, the Lamb of God. St. John the Baptist, of course, bestowed that title upon the Savior in their earliest exchanges when he saw the Lord coming toward him and proclaimed: "Behold, the Lamb of God, who takes away the sin of the world" (John 1:29).

The image of the unique saving Lamb has, however, further connections. In the Hebrew Scriptures we read of the slain lamb whose blood on the doorposts of Jewish homes saved the chosen ones as the angel of destruction "passed over" their homes. During subsequent centuries, God's special people annually remembered their deliverance with a Passover meal of a carefully selected lamb.

In the New Testament the first letter of Peter reminds us that we were saved, "not with perishable things like silver or gold but with the precious blood of Christ as of a spotless unblemished lamb" (1 Pet. 1:18). Christians carry in their minds and hearts this picture of Jesus, hanging on the cross, pouring out his blood for us and out of love for us. The Book of Revelation describes the Lamb as the one before whom those in heaven fell down in adoration, who could and would open the book of life. This book of life "belongs to the Lamb who was slain" (Rev. 5 and 13:1–10).

The breaking of the bread and the pouring of the cup have both practical and symbolic dimensions. Many grains of wheat are ground, kneaded, and baked together to become one loaf of bread. Similarly, many grapes are crushed, their common juice treated and aged to become one bottle of wine. In parallel fashion, we, though many different, unique persons, come forward to eat and drink of the one loaf and the one cup. St. Paul developed that famous metaphor in his first letter to the Corinthians: "Because the loaf of bread is one, we, though many, are one body, for we all partake of the one loaf" (1 Cor. 10:14–18).

To underscore that profound symbolic meaning, church directives encourage the use of bread and wine that truly have the appearance of food. Moreover, the regulations urge that the bread or host, although still unleavened, should be large enough so that the priest can divide it into a sufficient number of particles so that at least some of the people can receive consecrated pieces from the same host as the presiding priest. Finally, the church prefers that people receive the elements consecrated at the Mass in which they are participating and not from the tabernacle, carried over from previous liturgies.[71]

Worship directives also encourage giving participants the opportunity to receive Communion under both kinds, that is, both eating Christ's body and drinking his blood.

Making such substantial loaves of bread of only wheat and water, as regulations require, presents a real challenge. Dark-colored wines, red or pink, are more visible than white wines. Specially crafted glass vessels contribute to the visibility of the symbols, but they also chip and break. Estimating the number of communicants to determine the proper amount of bread and wine is likewise an inexact science. In other words, carrying out these directives and ideals requires effort and imagination.

THE MINGLING, OR MIXING

During the breaking of bread and singing of the Agnus Dei, the priest breaks off a tiny piece of the consecrated bread and drops it into the cup of consecrated wine. As he does so, he quietly says, "May this mingling of the body and blood of our Lord Jesus Christ bring eternal life to us who receive it."[72] That brief gesture, barely noticed by the congregation because of the distance and low tone of voice, embodies two historically symbolic meanings.

First, in the early Christian centuries, the Holy Father at his Mass often broke off several particles and sent them to neighboring churches and pastors. These priests received those consecrated pieces and then dropped them into their own vessels containing the Precious Blood. The gesture symbolized the bond of unity between the pope and his pastors.

Second, some spiritual writers have seen in the separate consecration of the bread and wine a symbolic dramatization of the crucifixion on Calvary. Since we receive the Risen Christ in Communion, with his body and blood reunited and transformed, it was thought necessary to dramatize prior to Communion this later reunion of Jesus' body and blood in the Resurrection. The mingling of the consecrated bread and wine, in this view, symbolizes that rejoining.

PRIVATE PREPARATION OF THE PRIEST

Following the breaking of the bread and the mingling of the elements, the priest joins his hands and says quietly one of two preparation prayers.

Since some priests either ignore or are ignorant of the directive to recite these beautiful prayers "quietly," they may distract the faithful who, according to Mass directives, are simultaneously preparing themselves by praying silently.[73]

INVITATION TO COMMUNION

After the quiet preparation for Communion, the priest genuflects in adoration before the Lord present on the altar, holds the cup with consecrated wine and the consecrated host above it, and then invites the people to Communion. The succinct invitation suggests three theological meanings:

- "Happy are those who are called...." The use of "those" introduces such mysteries as God's plan, free will, and grace. Why are some chosen and not others?

Many priests change the words to "we" who are called. This eliminates the points of mystery and could also inject a smugness or arrogance, although it should probably be considered rather as a vocalizing of gratitude.

- "...called to his supper." I wonder how many priests and people recognize this as a reference to the banquet still to come in heaven and to a particular text in the Book of Revelation: "Blessed are those who have been called to the wedding feast of the Lamb" (Rev. 19:9).

It also serves to remind us that the Eucharist is likewise a sacred meal in which we gather as a family and eat this spiritual food, the body and blood of Christ.

- The response of the people, "Lord, I am not worthy to receive you, but only say the word and I shall be healed," refers to the healing of the centurion's servant in Matthew's Gospel (Matt. 8:5–13). His faith, humility, and confidence are a model for all those baptized waiting to come forward to receive their Lord and Lamb in Communion and to experience his healing power.

Possible revisions would provide more variety and adaptability for these invitations, with the caution that the invitation always conclude with a recognizable cue so that the people can readily respond, "Lord, I am not worthy...."

PRIEST'S PERSONAL PREPARATION

In addition to the two prayers intended for the "Private Preparation of the Priest" prior to "This is the Lamb of

God...," the ritual adds for him a final personal preparation. This occurs after the "Lord I am not worthy..." and immediately before consumption of the consecrated elements. The church directs a priest to say, "quietly," this phrase: "May the body of Christ bring me to everlasting life." After he "reverently" consumes the blessed particle, the priest takes the chalice and, again quietly, says, "May the blood of Christ bring me to everlasting life."

Some priests recite this aloud, which both interrupts the congregation's silent personal preparation and may lead them to say "Amen" after his vocal rendition of these two beautiful petitions.

Procession for Communion

In most situations, people walk in a natural procession to the altar for Communion. This necessary action, however, can have symbolic overtones. We are like poor people waiting in line, slowly moving forward for a sandwich and cup of soup at some downtown church, a bag of groceries from an assistance office, or a ladle of porridge in an African refugee camp. We are like God's people in the past, alert, ready, and expectant, about to share the paschal meal and begin or continue the journey. We are like those same people confidently on the march toward the promised land.

Americans generally relish order, and that preference can impact our church services. Well-meaning ushers may want to stand in the aisle at the end of a pew or row of chairs, moving gradually backward one at a time, thus regulating the flow of people joining the procession for Communion. That makes for neat, military-like order, but a little reflection reveals how unwise and hurtful this process can be for noncommunicants. If persons have come back to Mass for the first time, or for whatever reason choose not to go to Communion, this procedure can isolate them, place them in the spotlight, and make them very uncomfortable.

Current directives for the United States establish standing as the norm for the reception of Holy Communion. Nevertheless, persons who kneel should not be denied Communion. Moreover, the norms direct communicants to bow their heads slightly in reverence when they come before the minister who is distributing to them the Body of the Lord or the Precious Blood.

RECEPTION OF COMMUNION

In the Hand or on the Tongue? In the first millennium, Catholic Christians usually received Communion in the hand and standing. St. Cyril of Jerusalem describes the fourth-century procedure in this section from his *Mystagogic Catechesis:*

> When you approach, do not go stretching out your hands or having your fingers spread out, but make the left hand into a throne for the right which shall receive the King, and then cup your open hand and

take the Body of Christ, reciting the Amen. Then
sanctify with all care your eyes by touching the Sacred Body, and receive it. But be careful no particles
fall, for what you lose would be to you as if you lost
some of your members.... [74]

During most of the second millennium the custom has
been to receive Communion on the tongue and kneeling.

The current practice, a blend of both previous prac-
tices, may well continue through the third millennium. In
most circumstances, communicants will be standing. Yet
in every circumstance, children and adults, female and
male, should have the option of receiving in the hand or
on the tongue.

However, in all situations the key attitudes must be
reverence and faith. The phrases "Body of Christ" and
"Blood of Christ" are statements and invitations. The
"Amen" on the part of the communicant means, "Yes,"
or "So be it," and could be well translated "I believe."
This "Amen" and a reverent bodily approach combine
to form an act of faith.

Communion from the Cup. Approaching the altar
to receive Communion continues our fulfillment of the
Lord's injunction to "Take and eat," "take and drink."
Thus, together we eat and drink the body and blood
of Christ. The greater sign of accomplishing this ideal
involves drinking from the cup as well as eating the
consecrated bread.

Luke's account of the Last Supper reminds us that "this
cup is the new covenant in my blood, which will be shed

for you" (Luke 22:20). Our drinking from the common cup means a deeper sharing in that covenant.

Matthew's account adds the prediction that, if we drink this cup with Jesus, we will one day share with Christ the heavenly banquet. "I tell you, from now on I shall not drink this fruit of the vine until the day when I drink it with you new in the kingdom of my Father" (Matt. 26:29).

Mark's account of James and John speaking with Jesus, seeking to sit in glory with Christ, one at his right and the other at his left, contains the Lord's subsequent warning and prediction: They will indeed have that reward, but only if they share in his cup of suffering and drink the chalice of pain with him. "The cup that I drink, you will drink..." (Mark 10:39). Drinking the Precious Blood from the cup gives us a deeper appreciation of being one with the suffering Christ, Jesus the abandoned one.

Offering the opportunity for everyone present to drink the Precious Blood from the cup is a currently encouraged ideal and a growing practice in parishes. However, the percentage of people taking advantage of that opportunity is relatively low, certainly less than a majority of worshipers.

A brief bit of history may be helpful here. The Christian church from the outset until the thirteenth century in the West (continuing on to the present in the East) consistently and commonly distributed Communion under both kinds to the laity. This was through those years and remains today the best expression and most perfect fulfillment of what our Lord said, did, and directed. At the same time, the church always gave Communion under one kind when circumstances so dictated and recognized this as a valid, complete, true sacrament. Thus the Eucharist was offered under the sign of bread alone to those confined to their homes, to the sick, to prisoners, or to monks living in isolation. Similarly, Communion under the appearance of wine alone for infants and the gravely ill formed a standard and accepted custom throughout this period.

Practical difficulties and poor attitudes linked to produce a change in the thirteenth and fourteenth centuries. There was no denial (in fact there was greater affirmation) of the truth that each kind — bread or wine — contained the "whole" Christ, present body and blood, soul and divinity, in all the fullness and power of his life, sufferings, and resurrection. But the faithful, for complicated historical reasons, approached the sacraments much less frequently and, unfortunately, failed to realize fully that sacrifice and sacrificial meal are one in the Mass. These doctrinal and devotional attitudes, combined with contagion in times of rampant disease, the possibility of irreverence or spilling, the hesitation of some communicants to drink from a common cup, the large numbers at Easter and other special feasts, and the scarcity of wine in northern countries, led to a gradual abandonment of Communion under both species.

A reaction set in during the fourteenth century and many reformers urged a return to the early Christian tradition. However, in doing so some maintained that Communion under the sign of bread alone was invalid, a deprivation, an incomplete and erroneous compliance with the Lord's teaching in John's Gospel. Roman Catholics — both clergy and laity — bristled during those heated days in the face of these attacks and discouraged or forbade reintroduction of the practice under such controversial conditions.

The bishops at the Second Vatican Council urged reintroduction of the cup under appropriate circumstances. An instruction of June 29, 1970, from the Vatican Congregation for Divine Worship implemented that directive:

> In order that the fullness of sign in the eucharistic banquet may be seen more clearly by the faithful, the Second Vatican Ecumenical Council laid down that in certain cases — to be decided by the Holy See — the faithful should be able to receive holy communion under both kinds. This leaves intact the dogmatic principles recognized in the Council of Trent, by which it is taught that Christ whole and entire and the true sacrament are also received under one species alone.[75]

It is very desirable, as a greater sign, that the communicant drink from the cup. But there is no obligation to do so, and the "whole" Christ is received under one sign alone, of bread or wine.

While intinction is permitted in the universal church, we generally do not follow this practice in the United States. For intinction the priest, deacon, or extraordinary minister dips the host into the chalice and says to the communicant: "The body and blood of Christ."

The communicant responds, "Amen." The difficulty with intinction is that it eliminates the option of Communion in the hand.

The church does not permit communicants receiving the host in their hands to then dip this consecrated particle into the cup. That practice eliminates the notion of drinking from the cup, increases the possibility of spilling drops of the Precious Blood, and creates the unsanitary prospect of communicants dipping their fingers into the consecrated wine.

Repeated scientific surveys have shown little danger exists of the spreading of disease through Communion under both kinds because of the presence of alcohol in the wine as well as the careful wiping and turning of the cup after each communicant.

Song, Cleansing, and Silence

Congregational singing during Communion can foster unity, express joy, and deepen spirituality. The singing is best done without books and may be interspersed with periods of silence and instrumental or choral music. Songs of adoration are better suited for benediction services than for Communion at Mass.

The cleansing of the sacred vessels is preferably accomplished after Mass and at the side, not on the altar and during the Eucharist.

A period of silence, a few moments without words, action, music, or movement, is highly desirable. It usually will be welcomed even by, or especially by, young people who have to move about a busy, noisy, and restless world. However, a song of grateful praise is also appropriate. The practice in parishes will vary.

PRAYER AFTER COMMUNION

After a period of silence, the congregation stands for the final Prayer after Communion. The priest sings or says that prayer from the *Sacramentary* and asks that the gifts, Christ's body and blood just received, will exert their positive effects upon all who have received them.

We have reached the end of the downward slope. We have given to God; God has given to us. The priest now sends us forth to bring the good news of Christ to others.

CHAPTER SEVEN

Concluding Rites

The Mass is brought to an end thus:

a) *The priest greets the people and gives them his blessing. On certain days and particular occasions he may expand this by including a special prayer over the people and a more solemn form of blessing.*

b) *Finally comes the formal dismissal of the people, who may now return to their daily lives of good works, praising and blessing God.*[76]

ANNOUNCEMENTS

Remaining at the presidential chair, the priest, deacon, or some other person makes whatever pastoral announcements are necessary. They should ordinarily be brief enough so that the congregation can remain standing without fatigue or restlessness. The announcements need include only a short sentence summary of the homily or theme of the Mass, a few remarks about important matters, and perhaps some words about the following week's Eucharist.

This part of the Concluding Rites should help the worshipers make a transition from their sacred encounter with God in Word and Sacrament to the world from which they came and to which they are returning.

BLESSING

The priest may give a simple blessing, but he is encouraged on Sundays, feasts, and major occasions to bestow a solemn blessing. The blessing both praises God and begs the Lord's divine protection.

The solemn blessings are threefold and invite the people's willing response by a strong "Amen" after each of the benedictions. The priest extends his hands over the people and makes a sign of the cross over them at the conclusion of the blessing.

DISMISSAL

The priest, or deacon if present, pronounces the dismissal, using one of several formularies. During part of the Easter season, a double Alleluia is added to dismissal.

This final message sends the people forth to praise and bless the Lord in the midst of their daily responsibilities. The people's response, "Thanks be to God," expresses their gratitude for experiencing Christ in the Liturgy of the Word and the Liturgy of the Eucharist.

If convenient, the priest kisses the altar before he joins the recessional. Eucharistic ministers to the sick may also join the recessional.

Song or silence are both effective for accompanying the ministers as they leave the church and for concluding the mystery of the Mass.

Notes

Preface

1. Kevin and Marilyn Ryan, eds., *Why I Am Still a Catholic* (New York: Riverhead Books, 1998), 17.

Chapter 1: The Mystery of the Mass

2. *The New Order of Mass* with introduction, commentary, and translation by Bruno Becker, O.S.B., and the Monks of Mount Angel Abbey (Collegeville, Minn.: Liturgical Press, 1970), *General Instruction of the Roman Missal,* article 1, p. 69.

3. John Jay Hughes, "Martin B. Hellriegel: A Priestly Man, a Manly Priest," *The Priest* (September 1981): 13–15.

4. Henri J. M. Nouwen, *A Letter of Consolation* (San Francisco: Harper and Row, 1982), 63–64.

5. Eileen Egan, *Such a Vision of the Street* (Garden City, N.Y.: Doubleday, 1985), 184–86.

6. *Vatican Council II: The Basic Sixteen Documents,* ed. Austin Flannery, O.P. (Northport, N.Y.: Costello Publishing Co., 1996), "Constitution on the Sacred Liturgy," article 2, pp. 117–18.

7. Ibid., articles 47–58, pp. 134–38.

8. *The New Order of Mass,* article 1, p. 1.

9. *Catechism of the Catholic Church* (Liguori, Mo.: Liguori Publications, 1994), 334.

Chapter 2: Changeless and Changeable Elements

10. *Vatican Council II: The Basic Sixteen Documents,* "Constitution on the Sacred Liturgy," article 21, p. 126.

11. Ibid., article 23, p. 127.
12. Joseph A. Jungmann, S.J., *The Mass of the Roman Missal* (New York: Benziger Brothers, 1959), 6–14.

CHAPTER 3: PLAN OF THE MASS

13. *The New Order of Mass,* article 8, p. 83.
14. Ibid.
15. *Vatican Council II: The Basic Sixteen Documents,* "Constitution on the Sacred Liturgy," article 56, p. 137.

CHAPTER 4: INTRODUCTORY RITES

16. *The New Order of Mass,* 103.
17. *The Sacramentary* (New York: Catholic Book Publishing Co., 1974), 359.
18. *Vatican Council II: The Basic Sixteen Documents,* "Constitution on the Sacred Liturgy," article 7, p. 121.
19. *The Sacramentary,* 362.
20. Ibid.
21. Ibid., 363.
22. Ibid., 363–66.
23. Ibid.
24. Ibid., 367.
25. Ibid., 360–61.
26. Ibid., 367.
27. Ibid., 368.
28. Ibid., *General Instruction of the Roman Missal,* article 23, p. 22.
29. Ibid., no. 32, "For the Sick," 916.

CHAPTER 5: LITURGY OF THE WORD

30. *Lectionary for Mass* (New York: Catholic Book Publishing Co., 1970), "Foreword," paragraph 33, p. 6.
31. Committee on the Liturgy, *Newsletter* (Washington, D.C., Secretariat for the Liturgy) 34 (February–March 1998): 9.

32. *Vatican Council II: The Basic Sixteen Documents,* "Constitution on the Sacred Liturgy," article 7, pp. 120–21.

33. Committee on the Liturgy *Newsletter,* 10.

34. Ibid., 5.

35. Ibid., 6 and 12.

36. Ibid., 6–7. See the entire June–July 1997 issue of the Bishops Committee on the Liturgy *Newsletter* for a detailed, informative, and fascinating account of this revision effort.

37. "Introduction," *Lectionary for Mass,* 9–10.

38. Ibid., 12–13.

39. Ibid., 9.

40. "Index of Readings," *Lectionary for Mass,* 1100–1116.

41. Ibid., "Foreword," 5.

42. *The Sacramentary,* 369.

43. Ibid.

44. Ibid.

45. *Vatican Council II: The Basic Sixteen Documents,* "Constitution on the Sacred Liturgy," article 52.

46. *The New Order of Mass,* article 41, p. 117.

47. *The Sacramentary,* 370.

48. Ibid.

49. Ibid., 141–55.

50. *Vatican Council II: The Basic Sixteen Documents,* "Constitution on the Sacred Liturgy," article 53.

Chapter 6: Liturgy of the Eucharist

51. *The New Order of Mass,* article 48, p. 123.

52. Ibid., article 8, p. 83.

53. Ibid., articles 49–53, pp. 125–27; *The Sacramentary,* 371.

54. *The Sacramentary,* 371.

55. Ibid.

56. Jungmann, *The Mass of the Roman Missal,* 333–35.

57. *The New Order of Mass,* article 51, p. 127.

58. Ibid., 40; *The Sacramentary,* 272.

59. Ibid., 40–41, article 52, p. 127; *The Sacramentary,* 372.

60. Ibid., article 53, pp. 128–29; *The Sacramentary,* 372.

61. *The Sacramentary,* 373.

62. Ibid., Eucharistic Prayer II, 549.

63. *The New Order of Mass,* articles 21–22, pp. 99–101.

64. *The Sacramentary,* 549.

65. Ibid., article 109, p. 32.

66. Ibid., 549–50.

67. *Vatican Council II: The Basic Sixteen Documents,* "Constitution on the Sacred Liturgy," article 34, pp. 129–30; article 50, p. 135.

68. *The Sacramentary,* 555.

69. Ibid., 562.

70. Ibid., 563.

71. *The New Order of Mass,* articles 281–85, pp. 261–85.

72. *The Sacramentary,* 563.

73. *The New Order of Mass,* article 56f, p. 135.

74. *The Mass of the Roman Rite,* pp. 508–9.

75. *Vatican Council II: The Conciliar and Post Conciliar Documents,* ed. Austin Flannery, O.P. (Northport, N.Y.: Costello Publishing Company, 1981), 206.

CHAPTER 7: CONCLUDING RITES

76. "General Instruction on the Roman Missal," in *Vatican Council II: The Conciliar and Post Conciliar Documents,* p. 179.

Of Related Interest
by Walter Cardinal Kasper

SACRAMENT OF UNITY
The Eucharist and the Church

For 2005, the Year of the Eucharist, Cardinal Kasper presents this comprehensive and rich explanation of the spiritual, pastoral, and theological aspects of the Eucharist, the center of Christian life and dialogue. The understanding of the Eucharist as sacrament of unity is not a peripheral or accidental matter. Indeed, the unity of the Church is the very reason the Eucharist exists.

0-8245-2314-8, $19.95 paperback

LEADERSHIP IN THE CHURCH
Theological Reflections

This book offers a timely and profound look at the enduring meaning of church office, and the guidance it is called to provide in light of a changed world and a challenging future. Topics addressed include: the universal vs. local church; the ministry of the bishop, priest and deacon; apostolic succession; and the practical application of canonical norms.

0-8245-1977-9, $24.95 hardcover

crossroad

Of Related Interest

Pope John Paul II
Edited by Carl J. Moell, S.J.
HOLY FATHER, SACRED HEART
The Complete Collection of John Paul II's Writings
on the Perennial Catholic Devotion

Pope John Paul II has given the devotion to the Sacred Heart a special place in his spiritual life and public ministry for decades. In *Holy Father, Sacred Heart,* Carl J. Moell, drawing from his experience working with the Society of Jesus in Rome, gathers together every teaching the Holy Father has proclaimed regarding this most intimate of Catholic devotions. From the Pope's speeches before audiences of millions, to his personal prayers and writings, *Holy Father, Sacred Heart* is the perfect treasury for everyone devoted to the Sacred Heart of Jesus Christ.

0-8245-2147-1, $24.95 paperback

Please support your local bookstore,
or call 1-800-707-0670 for Customer Service.

For a free catalog, write us at

THE CROSSROAD PUBLISHING COMPANY
16 Penn Plaza, 481 Eighth Avenue
New York, NY 10001

Visit our website at
www.crossroadpublishing.com
All prices subject to change.

crossroad